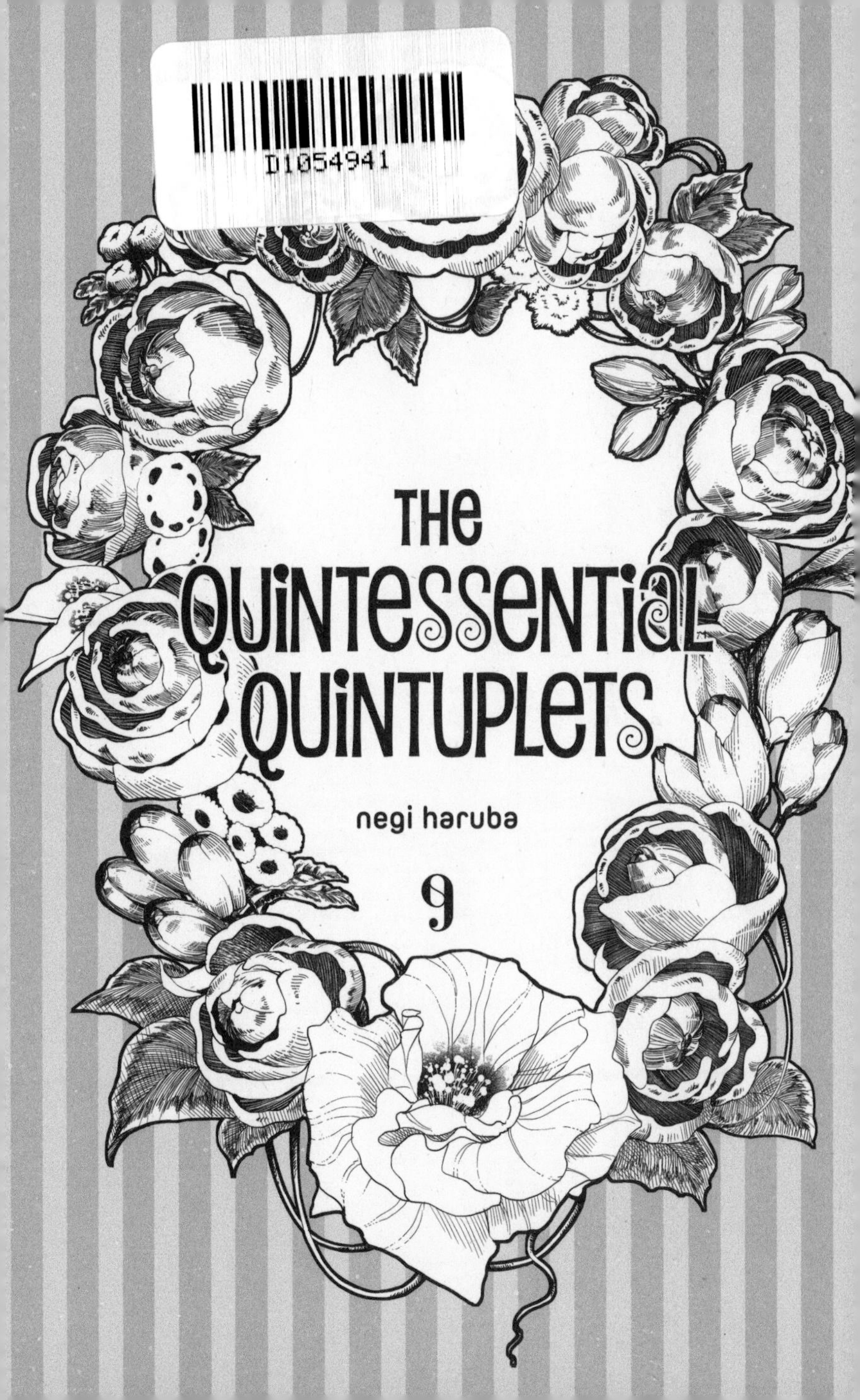
D1054941
THE
QUINTESSENTIAL
QUINTUPLETS
negi haruba
9

Character intros
HIS FUTURE BRIDE IS ONE OF THE QUINTS!!
NINO NAKANO
THE FIFTH SISTER. OR MAYBE THE FOURTH. THAT OR THE SECOND. YOU MIGHT THINK SHE'S THE THIRD FOR A MOMENT, BUT THE SECOND IS THE CORRECT ANSWER. SHE MUST BE THE SECOND. HER FAVORITE MOVIES ARE THOSE WITH YOUNG STARS.
ICHIKA NAKANO
THE FIFTH SISTER. NO, THE SECOND SISTER. OR SO YOU'D THINK, BUT SHE'S THE ELDEST SISTER. THE ELDEST IS THE MOST LIKELY OPTION. PROBABLY THE ELDEST. HER FAVORITE MOVIES ARE THOSE WITH FOREIGN CELEBRITIES.
Quints Memo
Hate to Study: If you try to teach them anything, they run.
Potential Flunkers: Their score on Futaro's quiz was 100 points...between the five of them.
On the Verge of Flunking: Had to change schools to avoid flunking out.
Very Idiosyncratic: The five sisters each have their own intense quirks, so dealing with them won't be easy.
...Guide the five of them to graduation!!

MIKU NAKANO
THE FIFTH SISTER. YES, THIS ONE IS THE FIFTH FOR SURE. MOSTLY THE FIFTH SISTER. SHE'S MORE FIFTH SISTER THAN THE FIFTH SISTER. REALLY THE THIRD. HER FAVORITE MOVIES ARE THOSE WITH WARLORDS.
YOTSUBA NAKANO
THE FIFTH SISTER. LOOKS LIKE THE FIFTH SISTER. BUT WHEN SHE SPEAKS, SHE'S THE FOURTH. WITHOUT A DOUBT, THE FOURTH SISTER. WE CAN CONFIDENTLY SAY SHE'S THE FOURTH SISTER. HER FAVORITE MOVIES ARE THOSE WITH SHARKS.
ITSUKI NAKANO
THE FIFTH SISTER. THE GENUINE FIFTH SISTER. 100%, WITHOUT A DOUBT THE FIFTH SISTER. THE BONA FIDE, AUTHENTIC FIFTH SISTER. BUT WHEN SHE SPINS AROUND ONCE, SHE'S NOT THE FIFTH SISTER. HER FAVORITE MOVIES ARE THOSE WITH DOGS THAT DIE.

FUTARO UESUGI
ONE BARBECUE MEAL.
MINUS THE BARBECUE.
THE QUINTUPLETS' PRIVATE TUTOR.WITHOUT ANY SHADOW OF A DOUBT, THE ELDEST SON. HIS FAVORITE MOVIES ARE...NONE IN PARTICULAR.
RAIHA UESUGI
NOW WE'LL ACTUALLY BE ABLE TO FILL OUR BELLIES, HUH, BIG BROTHER?
FUTARO'S SISTER. ELDEST DAUGHTER. HER FAVORITE MOVIES ARE THOSE WITH ZOMBIES.

The Quintessential Quintuplets

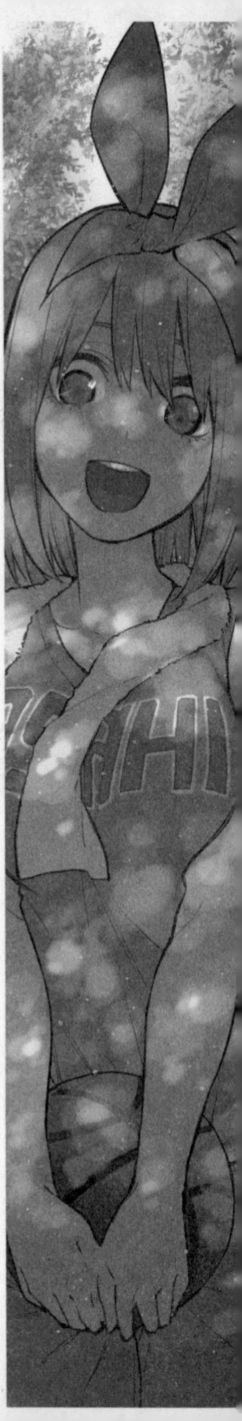

9

CONTENTS

CHAPTER 69
WELCOME TO CLASS 3-1

STARTING NEXT WEEK, WE'LL BE THIRD-YEARS, HUH?

201
Nakano

WE'LL BE THE HIGHEST GRADE IN SCHOOL...

I'M JUST GLAD WE MADE IT TO THE NEXT GRADE AT ALL.

LET'S DO OUR BEST THIS YEAR TOO, GIRLS!
YES, LET'S!

BY THE WAY, BEGINNING NEXT WEEK...

...WE WILL ALL HAVE TO SPLIT THE RENT EVENLY.

ANYONE WHO DOESN'T PAY...
...WILL BE SENT BACK TO OUR OLD APART-MENT.

NOW...
LET'S ALL WORK HARD IN ORDER TO STAY TOGETHER!

GOOD LUCK! ♡

A CONVENIENCE STORE... DELIVERING PAPERS...
THEY ALL SOUND TOUGH.
I WOULD FEEL A LOT BETTER IF WE COULD ALL WORK AT THE SAME PLACE...
NO ONE WILL HIRE THAT MANY EMPLOYEES AT ONCE.
AND WE'RE ALL GOOD AT DIFFERENT THINGS.

I DON'T KNOW WHETHER I CAN HANDLE CUSTOMER SERVICE...
WHAT IF A MEAN COSTUMER COMES IN?
MAY I HELP YOU?
YOUR FOOD GOT MY CLOTHES DIRTY!
YOU BETTER REIMBURSE ME OR I'LL CALL THE COPS!
I'M SORRY!
OR WHAT IF SOMEONE WORSE SHOWS UP...
YOU WITH THE RIBBON! GIMME ALL THE MONEY IN THE REGISTER!
EEEEEEEK!

I'M WITH THE POLICE, MISS. I'M HERE TO ARREST YOU FOR GETTING A CUSTOMER'S CLOTHING DIRTY.
HURRY UP OR I'LL SHOOT!
OH JEEZ! OH JEEZ!
WOW, EARNING MONEY IS HARD WORK.

BUT WE STILL NEED IT.
I NEVER EXPECTED ICHIKA TO SAY THAT NOW, THOUGH.

I WAS PLANNING ON FINDING WORK ANYWAYS, SO I'M GLAD I SAVED THESE WANT ADS.
...BUT...

...SEEING ICHIKA LIKE THAT REMINDED ME OF THE OLD DAYS.

OH, I THOUGHT THE SAME THING!
ACTUALLY, I THINK WE'VE BEEN LETTING ICHIKA TAKE ON TOO MUCH OF THE BURDEN ALONE.

YES. WHEN SHE GETS LIKE THAT, ICHIKA'S ONE TOUGH COOKIE...
AND SHE SAID WE'D BE FORCED TO RETURN TO THE OLD APARTMENT...
ALL ALONE THERE...

OR IT MIGHT BE JUST YOU AND DAD.
N-NOW *THAT* WOULD BE TENSE...

KNOW WHAT YOU'RE LOOKIN FOR, ITSUKI?
NO... I HAVEN'T DECIDED YET.
I'D LIKE A JOB I CAN REALLY SINK MY TEETH INTO...
...BUT IT'S HARD TO FIND ONE ON SUCH SHORT NOTICE...

SINK YOUR TEETH INTO?
YOU MEAN ONE THAT PROVIDES MEALS?
DON'T LUMP ME IN WITH HIM!
BUT I AGREE WITH YOU. I WANT TO FIND A JOB WHERE I CAN DO WHAT I LIKE.
WHAT I LIKE...
OH, SPEAKING OF UESUGI-SAN...
LOOK AT THE WANT AD I FOUND.

!
STAFF WANTED
¥900
is ¥1080.)
from 17:45 – 21:00.
ISN'T THAT...
...THE CAKE SHOP WHERE FUTARO WORKS?

WHUMP

NINO, GIVE ME THAT.
WHY? THIS IS MY AREA OF EXPERTISE.
WHY DOES IT HAVE TO BE THE PLACE FUTARO WORKS?
UGH...
THAT'S NOT WHY I WANT IT...

HEH HEH!
YES, THAT'S DEFINITELY NOT IT.

BUT YOU HAVE NO SENSE OF TASTE. YOU'D BETTER JUST QUIT WHILE YOU'RE AHEAD.

I WISH WE COULD ALL WORK TOGETHER!

WHAT ABOUT THIS CLEANING JOB, MIKU?
LET'S APPLY TOGETH-ER!
HRNGH ...

GULP...

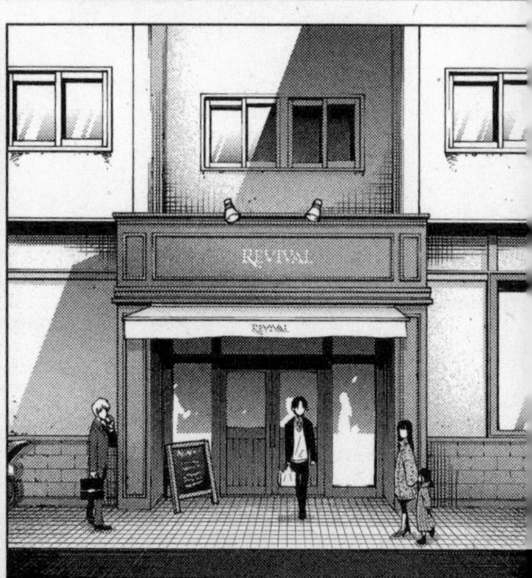
REVIVAL

AHEM, TODAY WILL BE THE IN-TERVIEW.
FIRST, JUST LET ME SAY I'M GLAD YOU SAW OUR AD.

...

BUT I CAN'T BELIEVE YOU BOTH CAME TOGETHER...

WHY DID YOU TWO APPLY HERE?!
I'D LIKE TO KNOW WHAT SHE'S DOING HERE, MYSELF.

I LIKE BAKING CAKES.
?!

I'D LOVE TO HIRE YOU BOTH IF POSSIBLE, BUT WE'RE BARELY SCRAPING BY, THANKS TO THAT CRAPPY BAKERY ACROSS THE STREET.
I CAN ONLY AFFORD TO HIRE ONE.
UNLESS OF COURSE UESUGI-KUN WERE TO QUIT...
AGAIN WITH THE JOKES, BOSS...
HA HA HA...
WHUMP

OH, THE YOU'RE BAKER

I GUESS THAT MEANS YOU'RE OUR-

W-WAIT A MINUTE! I'M A LOT BETTER THAN HER!

BUT SINCE THE BEGIN-NIGN OF THE YEAR, I'VE MADE TONS OF CHOCO-LATES.
ONLY BECAUSE YOU HAD MY HELP!
I MADE THE LAST ONE MYSELF.

UESUGI-KUN...
THOSE TWO ARE FRIENDS OF YOURS, AREN'T THEY?
HUH? YEAH, YOU COULD SAY THAT...

SO, YOU DECIDE
HUUUH ?!

WHO DO YOU CHOOSE, FUTARO?
HEY NOW...

NATURALLY, YOU'RE GOING TO PICK ME, RIGHT?
I'LL DO ANYTHING!

SO CHOOSE ME.

ALL RIGHT, YOU START NEXT WEEK.
CLANG-A-CLANG

I LOST...
...

YOU'RE THE ONE WHO DECIDED WE SHOULD HAVE A BAKE-OFF...
DID YOU REALLY THINK YOU HAD A SHOT?

BUT, WELL... I WON'T-

TMP

TMP

TMP

THE BAKERY ACROSS THE STREET IS HIRING TOO.
MAYBE I'LL APPLY HERE.
?!

YOU CER TAINLY MOVED QUICKLY.
YOU **DO** KNOW HE DOESN'T WORK HERE, RIGHT?!

YES.

MY GOAL ISN'T FUTARO.
!
WHEN I BAKED THAT CAKE JUST NOW...
...I FELT IT AGAIN.
HMM, THE FLAVOR ISN'T BAD, REALLY.
I GUESS I JUST LIKE COOKING.
WELL...
1
2
A good cook

...I'M GOING TO BECOME THE MIKU THAT FUTARO WILL FALL FOR.
...I WO THE BAKE-OFF...
...BUT SOME-THING DOESN'T SIT RIGHT.
STILL... I'LL USE THIS JOB...

...TO MAKE HIM FALL FOR ME.

...SO THAT'S WHAT HAPPENED.

HAHA...
I GUESS I KIND OF PUT EVERYONE ON THE SPOT.

WHAT ARE YOU DOING HERE, ANYWAY?
HMM? I FIGURED I'D ACCOMPANY MY LONELY FRIEND FUTARO-KUN...
...TO SCHOOL.

I'M NOT LONE-LY...
ANYWAY, I DIDN'T HAVE MUCH CHOICE.
UP UNTIL TODAY I'VE BEEN THE ONLY ONE WORKING TO PAY THE RENT...

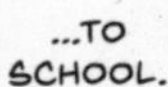

BUT NOW I WANT TO SPEND SOME TIME TRYING TO DO THE THINGS I WANT.

...
SO THAT'S HOW IT IS, EH?

IT LOOK LIKE EVEN YOTSU GOT HIRE
ALL THAT TRAINING CLEANING MY ROOM MUST'VE PAID OFF, HUH?
ITSUKI-CHAN SEEMS TO BE HAVING TROUBLE DECIDING, BUT I'M SURE IT'LL WORK OUT.
MAKES NO DIFFER ENCE TO ME
AS LONG AS YOU GIRLS KEEP YOUR GRADES UP.
AHAHA! AFTER ALL WE'VE GONE THROUGH, I DEFINITELY WANNA GRADUATE.
FWIP
I'M COUNTING ON YOU...
SENSEI!

NO, THAT WAS AN ACCIDENT...
BUT BACK THEN, WHAT WAS SHE...
NO, I'D BETTER JUST FORGET ABOUT IT.

YOU KNOW...

EVEN THOUGH IT WAS MY IDEA...
...THIS IS GONNA MAKE THINGS A LITTLE LONELY.
?

WE'LL ALL BE BUSY WITH OUR OWN THINGS.
I DOUBT ALL FIVE OF US WILL BE ABLE TO GET TOGETHER AS MUCH.

ARE WE JUST GOING TO GROW UP AND GO OUR SEPA-RATE WAYS?

BUT THAT ISN'T REALLY A BAD THING, IS IT?
RIGHT?!
BEATS ME.
I CAN SAY NOW...
...THAT WAS ONE CONERN THAT ENDED UP BEING COMPLETELY UNNECES-SARY.

WHAT CLASS'RE YOU IN?
NOOO! I'M NOT IN THE SAME CLASS AS MY BOY-FRIEND!

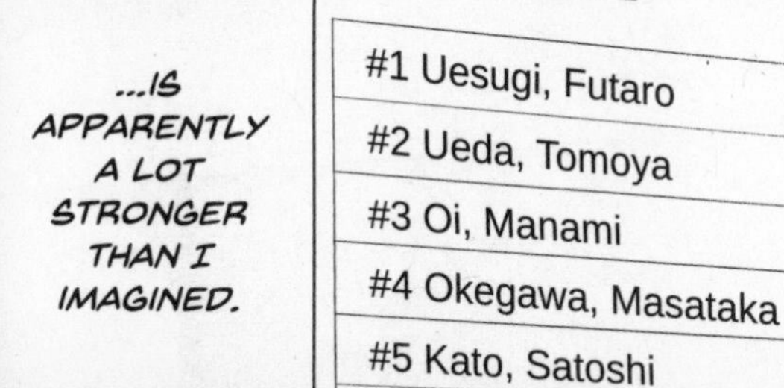

THE BOND THE SISTERS SHARE...
...IS APPARENTLY A LOT STRONGER THAN I IMAGINED.

Class 1

#1 Uesugi, Futaro
#2 Ueda, Tomoya
#3 Oi, Manami
#4 Okegawa, Masataka
#5 Kato, Satoshi
#6 Kamata, Shota

Tera

Tominaga,

Nakano, Ichika

Nakano, Itsuki

Nakano, Nino

Nakano, Miku

Nakano, Yotsuba

Nishioka, Kazuya

Hamamoto, Tetsuji

Hirakawa, Nobuo

THE QUINTU-PLETS!
I DON'T BELIEVE THIS...

I WISH THE ONLY THING THEY HAD IN COMMON WAS THEIR FACES.
3-1

CHAPTER 70
A CLASS OFFICER'S JOB

CHACK
SIR...
THE GIRLS WERE ALL SUCCESSFULLY ASSIGNED TO THE SAME CLASS.

AND?

HE IS IN THE SAME CLASS AS WELL.

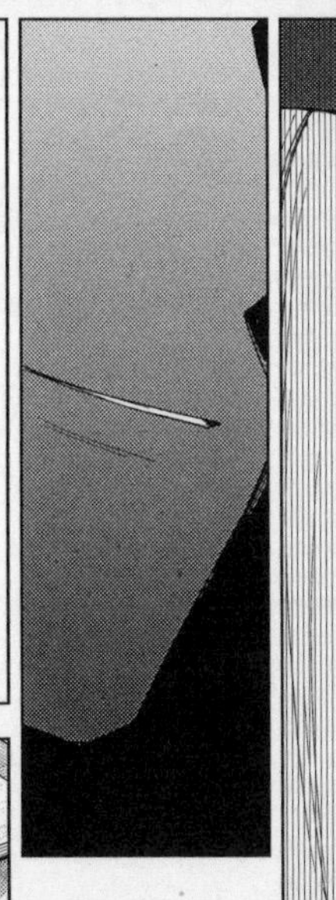

EXCELLENT WORK.
DING
DONG
MURMUR
MURMUR
MURMUR

CHATTER
MURMUR
MURMUR
CHATTER
CHATTER
MURMUR
BLAH
BLAH
BLAH
CHATTER
WOW!
I KNEW THE NAKANOS WERE QUIN-TUPLETS...
...BUT SEEING ALL FIVE OF THEM TOGETHER IS REALLY SOMETHING ELSE, HUH?
THEY LOOK EXACTLY ALIKE!

IT COULD GET COMPLICATED IF WE USE YOUR LAST NAME, SO CAN WE CALL YOU ALL BY YOUR FIRST NAMES?
SURE, THAT WOULD HELP US, TOO.
HEY, DO THAT THING!
THE TRICK WHERE YOU GUESS THE SAME CARD!
SORRY, WE DON'T HAVE TELEPATHY.

YOU LOOK JUST LIKE THE OTHERS, TOO, RIGHT, MIKU-CHAN?
GIVE ME A BETTER LOOK AT YOUR FACE.
...

STOMP
STOMP
YIKES!
SETTLE DOWN, EVERYONE!

LET ME THROUGH.

FUTARO.
H-HELP US, PLEASE.

HMM? ARE YOU INTER-ESTED IN THE QUINTUPLETS, TOO, UESUGI-KUN?

I'M GOING TO THE BATHROOM.
SO PLEASE GET OUT OF MY WAY.

HUH?
WHAT WAS THAT ABOUT?
HE'S SUCH A CREEP!

F- FUTARO.
FWISH

AHAHA... WE GOT IGNORED...
THE AME AS WAYS.

HE'S BEE LIKE THA SINCE LA YEAR.
IT'S LIKE HE TRIES TO AVOID GETTING INVOLVED WITH ANYONE IN CLASS.
HEY, YEAH! HE TRIED TO HANDLE HIS JOB ALL ALONE ON THE CAMPING TRIP, TOO!

HE'S THAT KIND OF PERSON.

I WISH WE COULD SHOW EVERYONE HE'S A GOOD GUY AT HEART.
IT'S HIS FAULT FOR ACTING LIKE THAT.

HEY, NAKANO-SAN, YOU'V TRIED THA ONE TRIC RIGHT?
THE ON WHERE YOUR SPI LEAVES YOUR BODY?

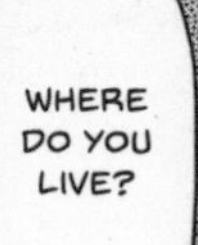
!

DO YOU EVER EN UP DOIN THE SAM THING AT SAME TI WITHOU PLANNI IT?
WHERE DO YOU LIVE?

WHY DON'T YOU TAKE YOUR "TRICKS" AND-
NOW, NOW...

THAT'S ENOUGH, EVERYONE.

DON'T YOU THINK?

EVERYONE TALKING TO THE NANAKOS AT THE SAME TIME MUST BE OVER-WHELMING TO THEM...
TAKEDA-KUN!
DON'T YOU THINK?
TH- THANK YOU...
YEAH, TAKEDA'S RIGHT.
WE GOT CARRIED AWAY. SORRY...
DON'T YOU THINK?
HA...HA-HAHA...
HANKS.
BUT I UNDER-STAND HOW EVERYONE FEELS.
EVERYONE WANTS TO KNOW MORE ABOUT YOU, SINCE YOU'RE QUINTUPLETS.

OH, THERE'S THE TEACHER.
IN YOUR SEATS
WE'LL NOW BEGIN ORIENTA TION.

WELL, I'LL TALK TO YOU AGAIN DURING THE NEXT BREAK.

GOSH!
TAKEDA-SAN IS SO NICE!
REALLY? HE SEEMS FISHY TO ME.
COME ON NOW.

STARTING TODAY, YOU ARE THIRD-YEARS.
I WANT YOU TO KEEP IN MIND THAT YOU ARE THE OLDEST STUDENTS IN THE SCHOOL AND CARRY YOURSELVES AS SUCH TO SET A GOOD EXAMPLE FOR YOUR UNDERCLASS...

...
UH, AND...

...WHAT IS IT?

BOOM
I VOLUNTEER TO BE...
...CLASS OFFICER!
HUH?
NO ONE ASKED YET...
CAN'T YOU HELP ME OUT HERE?! PLEASE LET ME BE THE CLASS OFFICER!
NO ONE SAID YOU COULDN'T, EITHER...
WELL, IF NO ONE ELSE WANTS THE JOB...
IF ANYONE HAS ANY ISSUES, THEY CAN COME TO ME FOR ANYTHING!
I GUESS WE CAN GO AHEAD AND CHOOSE THE MALE OFFICER TOO...
CLAP
CLAP
CLAP
CLAP
CLAP
CLAP
CLAP

DOES ANYONE WANT TO VOLUNTEER?
I'LL TAKE RECOMMENDATIONS AS WELL.
ANYONE?
THOSE TOO!
JEEZ, YOTSUBA...
HOW EMBARRASSING...
YOU DO IT.
NO WAY. ISN'T IT OBVIOUS WHO SHOULD BE THE MALE CLASS OFFICER?
IT'S GOTTA BE TAKEDA, RIGHT?
SOMEONE'LL RECOMMEND HIM EVENTUALLY.
HONESTLY...
I SUPPOSE I HAVE NO CHOICE.

SENSEI!
I KNOW SOMEONE WHO WOULD MAKE A PERFECT CLASS OFFICER!

SEE?

FUTARO UESUGI-SAN!
HUH?!
HUH?
UESUGI-KUN? REALLY?
SHE PASSED OVER TAKEDA-KUN FOR HIM...
WHO IN THE WORLD IS THIS GUY?
YOTSUBA... WHAT HAVE YOU DONE...?
ALL RIGHT, THEN LET'S MOVE ON TO THE NEXT POSITION-
SENSEI! I NEVER SAID I'D DO IT!

DAMN IT...
WHY'D YOTSUBA HAVE TO GO AND DO THAT...?

WHAT DO YOU WANT?
UESUGI-KUN...
IT SEEMS THE QUINTUPLETS TRUST YOU AN AWFUL LOT.
SO WHAT? BEING A CLASS OFFICER IS ONLY GOING TO GET IN THE WAY OF MY STUDIES...
HEH HEH HEH.

DON'T YOU THINK?

YOU HAVEN'T CHANGED ONE BIT.
THAT'S WHAT MAKES YOU MY RIVAL.

ONESTLY ...

ZSHHH

FUTARO.

DO YOU HAVE A SECOND?
I WANT TO ASK YOU SOMETHING.

WHAT IS IT, MIKU?

I HAVE HERE A MAGICAL LAMP.

I DON'T SEE ONE.
IT'S THERE.
?
IS THIS SOME KIND OF PSYCHO-LOGICAL TEST?
IF YOU HAD FIVE WISHES...
...WHAT WOULD YOU ASK FOR?

WHAT'S ALL THIS ABOUT?
IT IS A PSYCHO-LOGICAL TEST, RIGHT?
...
...WHO'S GOING TO ASK FOR ANYTHING BESIDES BECOMING RICH?
MONEY...
ARE WE DONE?
YOU HAVE FOUR MORE WISHES.
DON'T YOU USUALLY GET THREE?
HMM...

YOU CAN ASK FOR ANYTHING.
IT'S MAGIC.
WELL, I HAVE ALWAYS WISHED I HAD MORE STAMINA...
AND THAT LACK OF STAMINA LEADS TO EXHAUSTION, SO I COULD ALSO USE SOME-THING TO HELP WITH FATIGUE.
PLUS, I'VE HAD TROUBLE SLEEPING LATELY...
AND BETTER LUCK WOULDN'T HURT EITHER.
GOT WHAT?
THE TEST?
...
HUH? WHY AREN'T YOU SAYING ANYTHING?
TMP
TMP
TMP
...
GOT IT.
OH! THERE SHE IS!
SHE WAS OUT HERE THE WHOLE TIME!

nikuji (below) are a kind of good luck charm.

YOTSUBA-CHAN!
THE TEACHER WANTS TO SEE YOU!
UGH...
COME ON.
U-UM...
THIS WAY.

THAT'S NOT YOTSUBA.
SHE'S THE THIRD SISTER, MIKU.

NOD
NOD
HUH?!
REALLY?!

SORRY!
WE'RE STILL LEARNING WHO'S WHO.
NO BIG DEAL.
I'M USED TO IT.

TMP
TMP
TMP
OH!
THAT'S DEFINITELY YOTSUBA-CHAN!

HEY, THE TEACHER WANTS-
YOU'RE CLOSE!

JEEZ! HOW ARE WE SUPPOSED TO TELL THEM APART WHEN THEY ALL HAVE THE SAME FACE?!
GRR!
GRR!
GRR!

LISTEN HERE!!
IF IT'S TOO MUCH TROUBLE, JUST REMEMBER THE ACCESSORIES THEY WEAR!
LIKE THESE COMPLETELY LACKING-IN-STYLE HAIRPINS.
THAT'S WHAT I DO!
THAT'S AWFULLY RUDE...

YOTSUBA HAS THAT RIBBON THAT STICKS OUT LIKE A SORE THUMB.
REMEMBER THAT AND YOU WON'T MIX THEM UP.

NOT THAT I HAVE MUCH ROOM TO TALK...

YOU'RE AMAZING, UESUGI-KUN!
THANKS!

WHAT A SURPRISE! I GUESS YOU HAVE BEEN PAYING ATTENTION TO THE NAKANOS!
NO...
THAT'S NOT WHY...
I CAN SEE WHY YOU WERE CHOSEN TO BE CLASS OFFICER!

TELL US MORE ABOUT THE QUINTS!
HUH?
COME WITH US!
THERE'S ANOTHER ONE OVER THERE.

PLUNK
ぽつーん
HEY, YOTSUBA-CHAN!
NO, THAT'S NINO!

THOSE GIRLS...
THEY'RE ALL OVER FUTARO...
HEH HEH! WHAT'S THE PROB-LEM?
I'M SURE...
...HE'S CHANGING TOO.
I GUESS IT WAS NO MISTAKE THAT YOTSUBA RECOM-MENDED HIM.

BUT I CAN UNDER-STAND...
...WHY YOU WOULD BE A LITTLE JEALOUS.
!
WHUMPH
A-AS A FRIEND!

THERE'S SOMETHING WRONG WITH YOU...
FALLING IN LOVE WITH SOMEONE LIKE HIM...
OH, RIGHT.
I MANAGED TO ASK FUTARO HIS FIVE WISHES.
HE WANTS TO BE RICH.
BETTER SLEEP AND LESS FATIGUE...
HE WANTS MORE STAMINA.
HOW ARE WE SUPPOSED TO GIVE HIM BETTER LUCK?
NOT ONE WAS WHAT WE WERE LOOKING FOR, EH?
WHAT SHOULD WE DO?
EITHER WAY, WE'D BETTER HURRY, RIGHT?
YEP.
IT'S NOT LONG...

...UNTIL FUTARO'S BIRTHDAY!

OFFICER UESUGI! I NEED TO TALK TO MIKU-CHAN.

CLASS OFFICER, CAN YOU GIVE THIS TO ICHIKA-CHAN?

TO NINO-CHAN.
TO ITSUKI-CHAN.
AHHH!
WHAT A PAIN IN THE ASS!

CHAPTER 71
ADVANTAGE

3-1
AHEM, NOW THAT WE ARE THIRD-YEARS-
EXCUSE ME!
THAT JERK... WHY DOES HE KEEP PESTERING ME?
WE WOULD LIKE TO DISCUSS THAT WHICH COULD EASILY BE CALLED THE MAIN EVENT OF THE FIRST TERM!
YES, IT'S ABOUT TO START...

I CAN'T HEAR WHAT YOU'RE SAYING.
IT WOULD HELP IF YOU SPOKE A LITTLE LOUDER.

DON'T YOU THINK?

THE NATIONAL MOCK EXAM!
THE FIELD TRIP!

LET'S HAVE THE BEST TIME EVER, EVERY-ONE!
HUH? THAT'S THE ONE WE'RE TALKING ABOUT?
POKE
POKE

DO YOU HAVE WORK AFTER SCHOOL, NINO?
YES, I START TODAY.
SINCE YOU'LL BE AROUND FUTARO, TRY TO FIGURE OUT WHAT PRESENTS WE SHOULD GET HIM.
UH?
I NEED A FAVOR.
!
YOU'RE NOT GOING TO ASK ME TO TRADE WITH YOU ALREADY, ARE YOU?

ME? YO
SURE?
YES.
I START WORK TODAY, TOO.
I WANT TO DO EVERY-THING WE CAN TO MAKE SURE HE LOVES OUR GIFTS.

IT DOESN'T LOOK LIKE MIKU OR ICHIKA HAVE MADE A MOVE YET.
BUT HERE THEY ARE LETTING ME TAKE CHARGE... THEY MUST BE PRETTY CONFIDENT.
A LOT HAPPENED DURING THAT TRIP OVER SPRING BREAK...
BUT I... SHOULD BE...IN THE LEAD...

SO WHY...AM I SO UNEASY?

"THAT NEVER HAPPENED WITH ME."

I TOLD HIM HOW I FEEL ABOUT HIM, SO THERE'S NO WAY THAT'S NOT IN THE BACK OF HIS MIND, RIGHT?

OH.
YOU START TODAY?

Y-YES.
I THINK HE'S GOING TO LET ME RIGHT IN THE KITCHEN.

HEY, WHA DO YOU THINK O THIS HAI STYLE?
W-WELL, LOOKS LIKE IT'LL BE GOOD FOR WORK.
...

DON'T MESS IT UP.
HMPH!
WHO DO YOU THINK I AM?
I CAN DO THIS JOB WITH MY EYES CLOSED!

HEH HEH HEH...
YOU MAY HAVE HANDLED THE CHORES, BUT YOU'RE STILL JUST A SPOILED RICH GIRL.
I CAN'T WAIT FOR YOU TO LEARN THE HARSH REALI-TY OF WORK... OF THE REAL WORLD!
RMB
RMB
RMB

WONDER-FUL!
IT'S PER-FECT!

Très bien
I CAN'T BELIEVE YOU'RE MAKING DISHES LIKE THIS ON YOUR FIRST DAY! YOU'RE A REAL PRODIGY!
OH, REALLY? I THINK YOU'RE SIMPLY AN EXCELLENT TEACHER, SIR.
...

ZOOM
I FEEL FURTHER AWAY FROM HIM THAN EVER...
MAYBE I SHOULDN'T HAVE TOLD HIM...

WOW, IT'S GOING TO BE A HUGE HELP THAT YOU JOINED US, NAKANO-SAN.
WE'VE GOT AN IMPORTANT RESERVATION FOR TONIGHT.
OH RIGHT, YOU DID CALL THE ENTIRE STAFF IN TODAY. EVEN THE PART-TIMERS.
IS THERE A BIG GROUP COMING OR SOMETHING?
NO.
ONLY ONE PERSON.

M-A-Y.

A REVIEWER KNOWN TO EVERYONE IN THE BUSI-NESS.
SHE HIDES HER FACE, AND NO ONE KNOWS HER TRUE IDENTITY.

BUT HER REVIEWS ARE SO ACCURATE THEY SAY YOUR COSTUMERS WILL INCREASE IN PROPORTION TO THE NUMBER OF STARS SHE GIVES YOU ON REVIEW SITES.
M·A·Y

SHE'S EVEN VISITED OUR SHOP FROM TIME TO TIME IN THE PAST AND, EACH TIME, SAVED US FROM OBLIVION.
TONIGHT WILL BE HER FIRST VISIT WITH A RESERVATION. WE CANNOT FAIL.
ゴク… GULP…

SHE WANTS TO TRY OUR NEW SPRING DISH!
WE'RE SHOOTING FOR FIVE STARS!
YES, SIR!

I'VE GOTTA GIVE IT MY ALL!

I'M GOING TO BECOME A TRUE MEMBER OF THIS SHOP'S STAFF AS SOON AS POSSIBLE...
...AND GET CLOSER TO FUTARO!
EXCUSE ME? WHO MADE THIS DOUGH?
OH, THAT WAS ME.
BOSS.
IT TASTES A LITTLE FUNNY...
HUH?
UH-OH!
MAKE IT OVER AGAIN QUICK!
YES, SIR!

I'M TAKING MY BREAK.
OKAY.
YOU SHOULD TAKE ONE WHILE THERE'S TIME, TOO, NAKANO-SAN.
NO, I CAN KEEP GOING.
PLEASE LET ME KEEP AT IT!

...
M-A-Y-SAN WILL BE HERE SOON.
YOU'D BETTER REST WHEN YOU'VE GOT THE CHANCE.

I KNOW TODAY WAS ESPECIALLY HARD, SINCE YOU JUST STARTED.
SORRY.

...ALL RIGHT... YES, SIR...
THUNK

WHAT'LL I DO?
EVERYONE WAS SO BUSY BECAUSE OF ME...
I THINK I'D BETTER GO BACK AND-
I KNOW THE BOSS ALREADY SAID THIS, BUT THAT WASN'T YOUR FAULT.
IN FACT, IT'S 100% HIS FAULT FOR LEAVING IT IN A NEW HIRE'S HANDS.
HUNK

BUT, NORMALLY, THAT WOULD BE A PIECE OF CAKE...
WHY DID IT HAVE TO BE TODAY OF ALL DAYS THAT I MAKE A-
CHACK

OF COURSE I HAD TO SCREW UP SO BADLY WHEN FUTARO WAS AROUND...

CHACK

HERE, TAKE A LOOK AT THESE.
BUT MAYBE NOT TOO LONG A LOOK.
?
BACK DURING CHRISTMAS, I ACCIDENTALLY ORDERED 1,000 OF THESE SANTAS INSTEAD OF 100.
THE SHOP WON'T HAVE TO ORDER MORE FOR ANOTHER DECADE.

HUH
OH, AND THIS SCRATCH ON THE DESK?
I PUT THAT THERE WHEN I FELL.

WH-
WHAT ARE YOU TALKING ABOUT?

I'VE CARRIED THE WRONG CAKES TO CUSTOMERS' TABLES...
I CAN'T EVEN COUNT HOW MANY PLATES I'VE SHATTERED...
COMPARED TO ALL THAT, THIS IS A MINOR MISTAKE.

ARE YOU...

...TRYING TO CHEER ME UP?
N-NOT A CHANCE. I WAS JUST TEACHING YOU HOW HARSH THE WORKING WORLD IS.

AFTER ALL, I DO HAVE...
...MORE EXPERIENCE...
BUT WHY...
WHY IS HE AVOIDING ME?

OH...
SORRY FOR MAKING YOU WORRY ABOUT ME.
I KNOW T'S HARD BEING AROUND ME.

I'VE EXPERI- ENCED A LO OF PART-TIM JOBS...
...BUT EACH TIME, I ALWAYS COME BACK TO ONE THING...

I'M ONLY GOOD FOR STUDYING.
!

I'M JUST A SMART GUY...
WHO'S AT THE TOP OF HIS CLASS...
THAT COULD MANAGE TO TUTOR FIVE OF HIS CLASS- MATES AT ONCE. THAT'S ALL...
I THINK YOU'RE TOO CONFI- DENT IN THAT ONE AREA...

ALL I'VE EVER THOUGHT ABOUT WA STUDYING
I GAVE UP ON ALL HUMAN RE- LATIONSHIPS OUTSIDE MY FAMILY...

...THE FIRST TIME ANYONE HAD EVER ASKED ME OUT, SO...
SO THAT WAS A FIRST FOR ME.

...I DIDN'T KNOW WHAT TO SAY TO YOU.
BUT I'LL ANSWER YOU NOW.
I–
WAIT.

I KNOW YOU DON'T LIKE ME BACK.
AFTER ALL, I WAS HARD ON YOU ALL THAT TIME.
WE'RE FINALLY WORKING TOGETH-ER...
...BUT I HAVEN'T SHOWN YOU ANYTHING YET.

BUT DON'T DECIDE YET.
I WANT YOU TO LEARN MORE ABOUT ME.

I WANT YOU TO SEE...
...HOW MUCH I LOVE YOU.
THUMP
THUMP
OH, YEAH?
POOF
GOOD TIMING, YOU TWO!
M-A-Y-SAN'S ARRIVED!

ROGER THAT.
I'LL GO RIGHT AWAY.
WHAT'S THE MATTER, UESUGI-KUN?

YOU'RE RED AS A BEET.
!
OH!
THIS IS NOTHING–

I HOPE YOU'RE READY FOR IT...
FU-KUN. ♡

THAT'S M-A-Y-SAN...
WHO'S GOING TO TAKE HER ORDER?
YOU GO.
NO WAY, I'M SCARED AS HELL.

WHERE IS SHE?
OVER THERE. TABLE THREE...
SPROING!

HEH
HEH
HEH!
UM!
I'LL TAKE HER ORDER!
THAT NAKANO-SAN'S IMPRESSIVE...
SHE'S GOT GUTS FOR A ROOKIE...

SMOOCH
...!
WE'RE ON THE CLOCK, YOU KNOW...
NO, COULDN'T BE...

CHAPTER 72
RUMORS
HUH? YOU FORGOT TO ASK HIM ABOUT HIS BIRTHDAY?
DIDN'T YOU HAVE WORK WITH HIM?
YES, HE WAS THERE, TOO.
WHAT WERE YOU DOING?
HMM?
WHAT DO YOU THINK WE DID?
DO YO THINK SOMETH GOOD HAPPE NED?
SHE'S ACTING SO HAPPY.
I DON'T THINK FLAT-OUT ASKING WHAT HE WANTS IS THE BEST OPTION ANYWAY...
I KNOW!
I'LL ASK THE CLASS!

HUH?
WHO'S UESUGI?
YOU KNOW, THE CLASS OFFICER.
OH, THAT'S HIS NAME?
THEY'VE LREADY RGOTTEN HIM!

A PRES-ENT FOR UESUGI-KUN, EH?
HMM... I HAVE NO IDEA.
OH YEAH! I HEARD SOMETHING, YOTSUBA-CHAN.
IS IT TRUE...
HE DOESN'T SEEM THE TYPE TO ACCEPT PRESENTS.
DON'T YOU THINK?
ME EI-THER.
YOU DON'T?

...THAT YOU AND UESUGI-KUN ARE GOING OUT?

YOU'RE BOTH CLASS OFFICERS, AND YOU SEEM TO GET ALONG PRETTY WELL.
OF COURSE SOMEONE WAS GONNA GET SUSPICIOUS WHEN YOU RECOMMENDED HIM LIKE THAT.
AFTER ALL, WHERE THERE'S SMOKE, THERE'S FIRE.
WHOA!
WHOA!

ME G-GOING OUT WITH...UESUGI-SAN?!
I WOULDN'T DREAM OF IT!
ARE YOU SURE?

HE MIGHT NOT BE TOO OPPOSED TO THE IDEA.
BANG
NAKANO-SAN...
6.9.
WOW, UNDER SEVEN SEC-ONDS!
E'S A PEED MON...
10.5 SECONDS
HUFF
HUFF
IS THE P.E. OFFICER HERE?
HAVE THEM PUT THESE AWAY.
OH, EY'RE OUT ODAY.

THEN COULD YOU HANDLE IT, CLASS OFFICERS?
YES, SIR!
HUFF...
PUFF...
KH... HOW USELESS...
MEASURING OUR SPEED OVER 50 M WON'T AMOUNT TO ANYTHING...
COME ON. STOP COMPLAIN-ING.
LET'S JUST CARRY THESE BOXES TOGETH-
HE MIGHT NOT BE TOO OPPOSED TO THE IDEA.
IT MIGHT BE EASIER IF WE CARRIED SEPARATE ONES!
HUH?
YOU THINK SO?
THEN I'LL TAKE THIS HEAVY-LOOKING-
TUMP

I'LL TAKE THIS...HUGE ONE...
YOU HANDLE THE... SMALL STUFF...
KH!
HRNGHHH!
SHAKE
SHAKE
DON'T PUSH YOURSELF TOO HARD.

RATTLE
RATTLE
SEE? I KNEW IT!
THERE'S SOMETHING BETWEEN THEM FOR SURE.
ARE WE BEING WATCHED, OR AM I IMAGINING THINGS?
...
UM... I KNOW THIS IS A WEIRD QUES-TION...
BUT WHAT DO YOU THINK OF-

LOOKS PRETTY TOUGH THERE, CLASS OFFICERS.
WE'LL HELP.
ICHIKA... MIKU...
WEREN'T YOU ASKING ME SOMETHING, YOTSUBA?
NO! PLEASE FORGET I SAID ANYTHING!
CHATTER
CHATTER

BANG
ITSUKI!
TAKE OVER BEING CLASS OFFICER FOR ME!
HUH?!

BUT YOU WERE SO EXCITED ABOUT DOING IT.

PLEASE!
I'LL GIVE YOU A CRO-QUETTE ROLL!

I-IT'S NO USE TRYING TO TEMPT ME WITH FOOD!
AL-THOUGH I WILL TAKE THE ROLL!

THERE'S A WEIRD RUMOR SPREADING AND I DON'T KNOW WHAT TO DO.
SO I WANT YOU TO TAKE OVER FOR ME.

WHAT SORT OF RUMOR?
...

THAT ME AND...
...UESUGI-SAN ARE...D-DATE...S-SEE...
S-SEEING...TOGETH-ER...
OH!
LOOK AT THAT!
OH!
LOOK AT THAT!

SHEESH!
IF I HAD KNOWN THIS WAS GOING TO HAPPEN, I NEVER WOULD HAVE RECOMMEND-ED HIM!
HUMP

I DIDN'T WANT TO PUT THE OTHERS THROUGH THIS...
I JUST...

...WANTED EVERYONE TO KNOW HOW AMAZING UESUGI-SAN IS...
YEESH...
ALL THEY HAVE US DOING IS BUSY-WORK...
I'M THROUGH OVER HERE.
ARE YOU-
...
?

GIVE ME HALF.
!
WE'LL FINISH QUICKER.
U- UESUGI-SAN...
WHAT DO YOU THINK OF ME?
?
I HATE YOU.
HUH?

I-IT'S TRUE, TOO!
SO IT WOULD BE IN YOUR BEST INTER-EST TO STAY AWAY FROM ME!
OR ELSE...
S-
SOME-THING TERRIBLE WILL HAPPEN!
RIGHT ...

SO...
UM...
...
WHAT ARE YOU WORRIED ABOUT?

YOU AND ME GOING OUT?!

THAT'S THE ISSUE?
HOW COULD ANYONE THINK THAT?

NOT A CHANCE, RIGHT?
I-I KNOW...

BUT GIRLS LOVE TALKING ABOUT OTHER PEOPLE'S LOVE LIVES.
THERE'S REALLY NO GETTING AROUND IT.

LOVE, EH?
OH!

RIGHT... YO
DON'T LIKE
TALKING
ABOUT THI
STUFF, DO
YOU?
WHAT DID YOU CALL IT? THE STUPID-EST...
FURTHEST REMOVED ACT FROM ACADEMICS.
...AT LEAST...
...THAT'S WHAT I USED TO THINK.

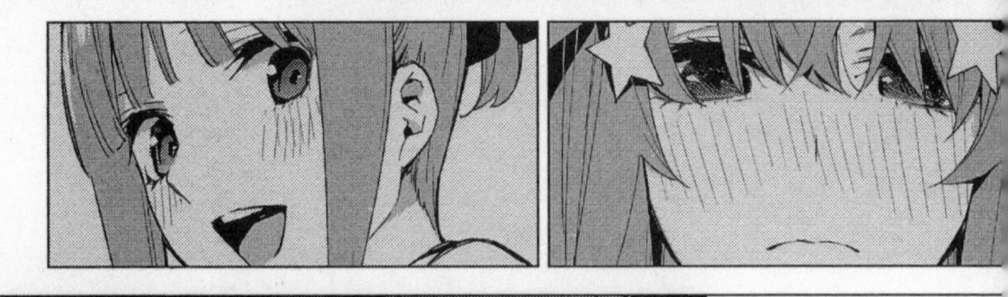

I NO LONGER FEEL MUCH LIKE MAKING FUN OF SUCH SERIOUS FEELINGS.

WHAT HAPPENED?
DON'T TELL ME YOU FINALLY FELL FOR SOMEONE YOURSELF?
HUH?

W-WAIT, YOU DON'T ACTUALLY LIKE ME, DO YOU?!
THAT'S NOT IT.

AND DON'T GO AROUND ASKING ABOUT IT!
HEH HEH HEH!
APPARENTLY, WHERE THERE'S SMOKE, THERE'S FIRE!

IT'S NOT LIKE THERE'S A CERTAIN SOMEONE SPECIAL I'M INTERESTED IN OR ANYTHING...
OH, REALLY? ARE YOU SURE YOU DON'T LIKE SOMEONE?

LIKE, MAYBE... MIKU?
!

WHY ARE YOU BRINGING UP MIKU?
HMM.
LOOKS LIKE THERE'S A LONG ROAD AHEAD...
BUT IT'S STILL A GOOD FIRST STEP.
PHEW!
I'M JUST GLAD YOU DON'T THINK LOVE IS STUPID ANYMORE.
WHO KNOWS? MAYBE YOU'LL TAKE AN INTEREST IN SOMEONE ONE OF THESE DAYS.
WHEN THAT TIME COMES, NO MATTER WHO YOU FALL FOR...
OR WHAT KIND OF ROMANCE YOU HAVE...
I'LL BE ON YOUR SIDE.

...YOU'RE GETTING WAY AHEAD OF YOURSELF.
AHAHA!
WELL, SINCE WE FINISHED OUR WORK, LET'S JOIN EVERYONE.

I'LL SUPPORT YOU WITH EVERYTHING I'VE GOT!
Y-YEAH.
I'VE GOTTA GO TO THE BATHROOM, SO YOU GO ON AHEAD.
HUH?
ALL RIGHT.
I DON'T MIND WAITING THOUGH. MAYBE IT'S NUMBER TWO?
Y-YOTSUBA-CHAN!
!

YOU WERE WITH UESUGI-KUN AGAIN, WEREN'T YOU?!
WE SAW IT!

ALL ALONE IN THE CLASSROOM AFTER SCHOOL!
EEK! HOW ROMANTIC!

SO YOU TWO REALLY ARE-
NO.

NOT EVEN A CHANCE.

O-
OH...

UESUGI-KUN?
YOU DO THIS EVERY TIME! WHAT DO YOU WANT?!
IT SOUNDS TOUGH...
...BEING THE NAKANOS' PRIVATE TUTOR.
HOW DO YOU KNOW THAT?
HEH HEH!
HOW ABOUT IT?
I WOULDN'T MIND TAKING YOUR PLACE. AND THAT WOULD BE QUITE A LOAD OFF...
...DON'T YOU THINK?

CHAPTER 73
THE NEW BATTLE OF KAWANAKAJIMA*

I HEARD THE WHOLE TALE FROM THE QUINTS' FATHER.
HE NEEDED SOMEONE TO PREVENT HIS STRUGGLING DAUGHTERS FROM FAILING...
...AND, AS YOU HAD THE TOP GRADES IN CLASS, YOU WERE THE LAMB SENT TO SLAUGHTER?
HOW DO YOU KNOW THEIR FATHER?

BECAUSE *MY* FATHER IS THIS SCHOOL'S CHAIRMAN.
I'VE BEEN ON FRIENDLY TERMS WITH THE NAKANOS' FATHE FOR YEARS.
BUNCH OF RICH BOYS...

BUT LET FORGE ABOUT THAT FOR TH MOMEN
IT SEEMS THIS IS NOT YOUR ONLY PART-TIME JOB.

THAT MUST BE TOUGH.
WHY DON'T I TAKE OVER FOR YOU?

*The original Battles of Kawanakajima were series of battles fought between 1553 and 1 between Shingen Takeda and Kenshin Ues

I'D LOVE TO LET YOU TAKE OVER.
BUT, UNFORTUNATELY, THEIR FATHER ISN'T THE ONE WHO HIRED ME. THEY DID. IT'S NOT MY DECISION.

OH?
QUITE THE CONFIDENCE YOU HAVE.
ARE YOU THAT CERTAIN THE NAKANOS WILL NOT LET YOU GO?
UGH!

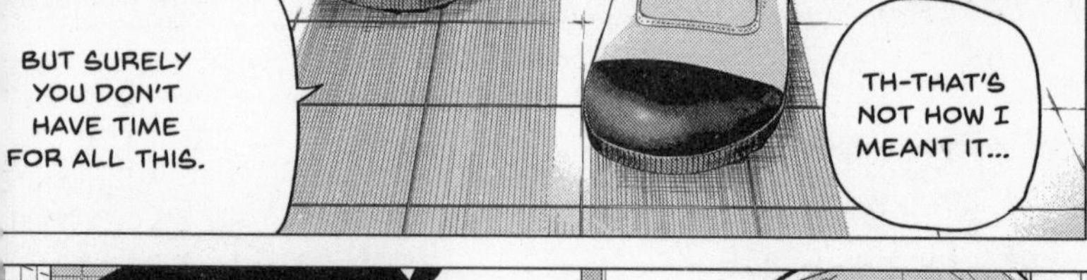
TH-THAT'S NOT HOW I MEANT IT...
BUT SURELY YOU DON'T HAVE TIME FOR ALL THIS.

DON'T YOU HAVE A MORE IMPORTANT USE FOR YOUR TIME?
?
WHAT ARE YOU GETTING AT?

HOW DISS-APOINT-ING
I HAVE NO FURTHER USE FOR A LIFELESS VERSION OF YOU.
I'LL JUST BE ON MY WAY.

THAT GUY...

IT'S BEEN A WHILE SINCE WE ALL STUDIED HERE.
WE'VE ALL HAD WORK LATELY.
ICHIKA'S GOT WORK TODAY, TOO.
I WISH I COULD'VE GONE TO THAT PREVIEW SCREENING WITH HER...
BY THE WAY...

ITSUKI, DID YOU FIND A JOB YET?
ERK!
WHAT? STILL?
PLEASE GIVE ME A LITTLE LONGER TO THINK IT OVER...
GIRLS, MOVE YOUR HANDS, OT YOUR MOUTHS!
THE NATIONAL MOCK EXAM IS COMING UP AT THE END OF THE MONTH!
FIN- SHED THIS ONE.

HERE, GRADE IT FOR ME...
FU- KUN!
FWIP

WHUMP
I FINISHED, TOO.
THE MOCK EXAM IS PRETTY TOUGH, HUH?
YES.
YOU'RE IN MY WAY...
WHAT DO YOU MEAN?
HUH?

BONK
BUT I'M NOT ES-PECIALLY WORRIED ABOUT IT, EITHER.
BONK
BONK
RIGHT?!
...YES, NOT AFTER WE CONQUERED FINALS.
WE'VE CLEARED THIS HURDLE BEFORE. THIS WILL BE A PIECE OF CAKE.
AT THIS POINT, IT'S LOOKING LIKE GRADUA-TION IS IN OUR SIGHTS! RIGHT, UESUGI-SAN?!
THEY AREN'T WRONG.
THE DIFFI-CULTY OF THE EXAMS ISN'T THAT DIFFERENT.
DOES THAT MEAN VICTORY REALLY IS IN SIGHT?
THE GOAL THAT ONCE SEEMED SO FAR AWAY?!
ALL RIGHT!
SIT BACK WHILE I GRADE THESE, GIRLS!
OKAY!

YOU'VE GOTTA BE KIDDING...

YOU FAILED ALMOST EVERY-THING...

STOP FOOLING AROUND...
ARE YOUR BRAINS BUILT TO RESET EVERY TIME YOU GO UP A GRADE?
OH, HEY! THAT EXPLAINS SO MUCH!

I THOUGHT I PASSED...
THIS MIGHT SOUND LIKE AN EXCUSE...
...BUT WE'VE ALL BEEN WORKING SO MUCH RECENTLY THAT WE DIDN'T HAVE TIME TO REVIEW ON OUR OWN.

NOW THAT YOU MENTION IT...
ITSUKI'S SCORE DIDN'T GO DOWN THAT MUCH.
I'M SORRY! I'M SORRY!

YOU WER JUST TALK ABOUT H EASY IT W GONNA B TO PASS NOW TH
AND I NEED TO STUDY FOR THE EXAMS MYSELF...
ALL RIGHT, LET'S GO THROUGH TH ONES YOU MISSED ONE BY ONE.
OKAY!
DING
DONG
!
COM-ING!
FUTARO, ABOUT THIS ONE–
CHACK
HUH?!

HELLO, GIRLS.
?!
D-
DAD?!
WHAT BRINGS YOU HERE?
IN FACT, DID WE EVER GIVE YOU THIS ADDRESS?
I HEARD THE NATIONAL MOCK EXAMS WERE SOON...
...SO I CAME TO INTRODUCE YOU TO SOMEONE.
COME IN.

PARDON ME.
MY APOLO-GIES.
I HATE TO STOP BY UNINVITED LIKE THIS...

HUH?
YOU'RE-
WHAT'S THIS ABOUT?
I-I'VE GOT NO IDEA WHAT'S GOING ON...

BEGINNING TODAY, TAKEDA-KUN HERE WILL BE YOUR NEW TUTOR.

!
HUH?!

WHAT DO YOU MEAN?
AN EXPLANATION, PLEASE?

UESUGI-KUN.

YOUR RESULTS ON THE PREVIOUS EXAM WERE IMPRESSIVE.
I HAD A TERRIBLE TIME WITH THESE GIRLS AND THEIR GRADES...
...BUT YOU TAUGHT ME THAT ENLISTING A SKILLED CLASSMATE COULD YIELD GREAT RESULTS.

THEN WHY CHANGE TUTORS?
OH...

I WOULDN'T IF HE WERE STILL THE MOST SKILLED CANDIDATE.

HUH?
UNFORTUNATELY, UESUGI-KUN'S GRADES FELL IN EVERY SUBJECT...
...CAUSING HIM TO EVEN DROP DOWN IN THE CLASS RANKINGS.

AND THE STUDENT WHO TOOK HIS PLACE AT NUMBER ONE IS TAKEDA-KUN.
SO HE IS THE ONE MOST SUITED TO BE YOUR TUTOR.
HEH!

HEH HEH HEH!

HEH HEH HEH...
HEE HEE HEE...

I DID IT!
I WON!
I FI-NALLY WON!
YES!
OH YES!
...
YES! YES! YES!

FWOOOSH
UESUGI-KUN!
TODAY ENDS OUR LONG-STANDING RIVALRY!
I HAVE FINALLY SURPASSED YOU!
I SHALL NOW TUTOR THE GIRLS!
...
IT ALL BEGAN TWO YEARS AGO...

WAIT, WHO ARE YOU ANYWAY?
HUH?
YOU KNOW...
YUSUKE TAKEDA, THE ONE WHO WAS ALWAYS RIGHT ON YOUR TAIL, IN SECOND PLACE...
IS THAT WHY YOU WOULDN'T LEAVE ME ALONE?
I HAD NO IDEA.
UNTIL NOW, I ALWAYS HAD PERFECT GRADES...
...SO I NEVER TOOK NOTICE OF ANYTHING BELOW NUMBER ONE.
SHOCK
ANYTHING BELOW NUMBER ONE ?!?!
BELOW NUMBER ONE...
HOW PITIFUL...

UNDER-
STOOD.

!
I DO NOT MIND IF YOU BELIEVE THE TOP STUDENT IN OUR GRADE IS MOST SUITED TO BE OUR TUTOR.

THAT PROBABLY ISN'T THE ONLY REASON...
"I HATE THAT BOY."

BUT, IN THAT CASE, I HAVE PLANS OF MY OWN.

I WILL GET THE BEST SCORE IN OUR CLASS!

HUH?
HUH?
HUH?
I SEE.

YOU HAVE A DEAL.
W-WAIT A SECOND!
IT DOESN'T MATTER WHAT YOU SAY, DAD!
WE HIRED FUTARO OURSELVES.
THAT'S RIGHT!
YOU ABANDONED US ALL THIS TIME! YOU CAN'T JUST WALTZ IN NOW AND-
HAVEN'T YOU REALIZED IT YET?
QUITTING HIS JOB AS YOUR TUTOR...
...WOULD BE IN UESUGI-KUN'S BEST INTEREST.

IT'S YOUR FAULT.
YOU ARE THE ONES WHO TURNED UESUGI-KUN NORMAL.

HE HAS HIS OWN LIFE TO LIVE.
WHY DON'T YOU SET HIM FREE?

...
BUT...

YEAH.
THAT'S EXACTLY RIGHT.

!
UESU-GI-SAN...

I GET THAT YOU HELD A HIGHLY INFLATED OPINION OF ME.
ND WHAT YOU'RE SAYING ISN'T WRONG.

BUT UNTIL LAST SUMMER...
...OR MAYBE IF I HADN'T TAKEN THIS JOB...
...I WOULDN'T HAVE TURNED INTO EVEN A NORMAL PERSON.
I THOUGHT I KNEW EVERYTHING JUST BECAUSE I HAD MEMORIZED ALL THE TEXTBOOKS.
BUT I HAD NO IDEA...
I HAD NO IDEA THERE WERE SUCH IDIOTS IN THE WORLD.
OR THAT I WAS SUCH AN IDIOT.
AS LONG AS THE GIRLS WANT ME, I'LL STICK WITH THEM.
THERE'S NO NEED TO RELEASE ME.

WHAT OBLIGATION DO YOU HAVE TO GO SO FAR FOR THEM?

NO OBLIGATION.
BUT...

THEIR GRADES WILL NEVER DROP AGAIN.
AND WHILE I APOLO-GIZE FOR WORRYING YOU ABOUT MY OWN FALLING GRADES...
I KNOW FOR A FACT THAT I'M THE ONLY ONE WHO CAN DO THIS JOB!!
...I SHALL DEFEAT HIM...
...REGAIN MY PLACE AT THE TOP OF OUR GRADE...

...AND TAKE FIRST PLACE ON THE NATIONAL MOCK EXAM!
AND!
WHUMP
U-UESUG SAN?
WHAT?!
NUMBER ONE ON THE NATIONALS IS TOO RECK-LESS!
BE MORE REALISTIC, FUTARO...

HUH?! BUT JUS BEING NUMBE ONE AT SCHOO ISN'T ANY DIF-FERENT FROM BEFORE!
JUST LISTEN TO US!

HE'LL MAKE IT INTO THE TOP TEN ON THE NATIONAL EXAM!
HOW ABOUT THAT?!
HEY! LET GO!
SKREEEEEEEK

...
HE WENT BIG.

OF COURSE IT'S IMPOS-SIBLE.
YOU CAN'T PULL THAT OFF WHILE TEACHING THE FIVE OF THEM.

VERY WELL.

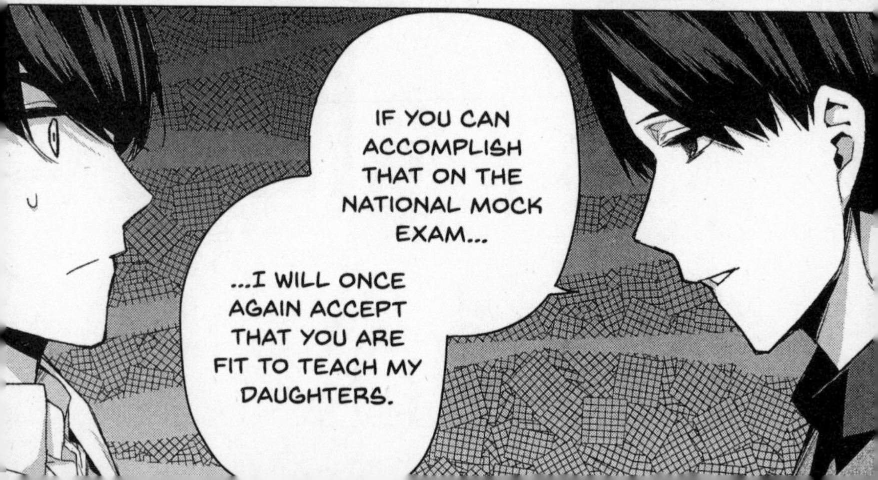
IF YOU CAN ACCOMPLISH THAT ON THE NATIONAL MOCK EXAM...
...I WILL ONCE AGAIN ACCEPT THAT YOU ARE FIT TO TEACH MY DAUGHTERS.

CHAPTER 74
THROWING A CURVE BALL
RMB
RMB
RMB
RMB
RMB
RMB
RMB
MUTTER MUTTER MUTTER
MUTTER MUTTER MUTTER
National Mock Exam
FUTARO-KUN!
YOU'D BETTER WATCH YOUR STEP.
MORNING!

ICHIKA, EH?
I'VE BEEN RUNNING INTO YOU ON AN UNUSUAL NUMBER OF MORNINGS LATELY.
YOU AREN'T WITH YOUR SISTERS?
HUH?! OH, UH... I CAME TO BUY THIS!
IT'S ONLY A COINCIDENCE I RAN INTO YOU! ONLY A COINCIDENCE! AHAHAHA!
OH YEAH! THIS IS FOR YOU.
YOU HAD THAT READY EVEN THOUGH YOU ONLY RAN INTO ME BY CO-INCIDENCE?
BUT I DON'T DRINK COF-FEE...
IT'S TOO BITTER...
TH-THEN I'LL DRINK IT!
YUM YUM!
GLUG
GLUG

COME ON. LET'S HURRY BEFORE WE'RE LATE.
...

SIGH, I GUESS I TRIED BUT...
...MY BRIBERY PLAN FAILED, TOO.
STILL, THERE'S ABSOLUTELY NO WAY I CAN USE A STRAIGHT-FORWARD APPROACH...
...PUT-TING ONE RIGHT OVER THE PLATE, LIKE NINO!!
BUT...

I DON'T WANT TO GIVE THIS POSITION UP TO ANYONE.

I HEARD FROM THE OTHERS.

YOU HAD ANOTHER ISSUE WITH DAD?

YEAH. HOW MANY TIMES HAVE WE FOUGHT OVER WHETHER I'M QUITTING OR NOT?

AND THIS TIME YOU'RE UP AGAINST TAKEDA-KUN, RIGHT?

!
YOU KNOW HIM?

WE HAD CLASS TOGETHER LAST YEAR.
HE HAD THIS KIND OF "FINE YOUNG MAN" THING GOING FOR HIM.
ALTHOUGH THAT SEEMS TOUGH IN ITS OWN WAY.

...
IT DOESN'T MATTER WHO I'M UP AGAINST. I HAVE NO INTENTION OF LOSING.
WE'RE STUDYING NONSTOP UNTIL THE EXAM AT THE END OF THE MONTH. BE READY.
U-US TOO?

HIS BIRTH-DAY'S JUST AROUND THE CORNER, BUT NOW IT'S HARD TO BRING IT UP...
UT...

...UNLIKE YOUR SISTERS, YOU'VE BEEN STUDYING AND WORKING AT THE SAME TIME SINCE FINALS.
I'M NOT WORRIED ABOUT YOU.

HEH HEH HEH.
YOU'VE GOTTEN GOOD AT HANDLING THE LADIES, HAVEN'T YOU?
HMM? HAVE YOU ALWAYS WORN GLASSES?
TOOK YOU LONG ENOUGH TO NOTICE!
I TAKE IT BACK... YOU'RE STILL MR. OBLIVIOUS...
I WAS HOPING YOU'D NOTICE EARLIER.

SO?
DO THEY MAKE ME LOOK MORE INTELLECTUAL?

THEY'RE KIND OF LIKE A DISGUISE.
A DIS-GUISE ...

YOU KNOW, THERE WAS A PREVIEW SCREENING OF THAT MOVIE I WAS IN YESTER-DAY...
AND IT WAS PICKED UP ON A FEW TV STATIONS...

D-DO YO
REMEMB
IT?
THUMP
THUMP
IT'S THE MOVIE WE WERE FILMING THAT DAY...
!
SHAKE
SHAKE
SHAKE

HEH HEH HEH..
YOU'RE IN DISGUISE SO YOU DON'T GET MOBBED BY FANS?
YOU'RE A REAL STAR, AREN'T YOU?
JEEZ! STOP! YOU'RE EM-BARRASSING ME!

HEH HEH HEH... BUT I GUESS DISGUISES ARE YOUR SPECIALITY AS A GROUP.
OH, THAT'S A GOOD POINT.
WE'RE ALWAYS PREPARED FOR JUST SUCH AN OCCASION.
I CAN DO YOTSUBA OR MIKU IN THE BLINK OF AN EYE.
OH!
AND NOW I CAN DO NI-

...

AHAHA!
BUT IF I DID THAT, YOU WOULDN'T BE ABLE TO TELL WHO I AM, SO I'D BETTER NOT.

HMPH, DON'T UNDER-ESTIMATE ME.

JUST THE OTHER DAY, I SAW THROUGH EVEN MIKU'S DISGUISE, WITH NO HINTS.
!

WAIT, YOU MEAN-
HMM?

AREN'T THOSE YOUR SISTERS?

LOOKS LIKE WE CAUGHT UP TO THEM.

LET ME SHOW YOU HOW HILARIOUSLY WRONG YOU ARE.
HEY NOW, ITSUKI'S EATING AGAIN.
AND YOTSUBA'S TALKING SO LOUDLY.
STOP...

I WAS REALLY SURPRISED WHEN NINO GOT A JOB AT THE SAME PLACE AS ME.
BUT I WAS EVEN MORE SURPRISED WHEN I HEARD MIKU GOT ONE AT THE BAKERY ACROSS THE STREET.
PLEASE STOP...
OUR BOSS WAS PRETTY HAPPY, THOUGH. THEY STOPPED GETTING AS MANY CUSTOMERS.
DON'T TALK ABOUT OTHER GIRLS.

WAIT.
WHY...

WHY WON'T HE JUST PAY ATTENTION TO ME?!

HEY.
WHY DON'T THE TWO OF US PLAY HOOKY TODAY?
!
THUMP
THUMP

YOU KNOW WE CAN'T.

AW, COME ON! JUST FOR TODAY!
WEREN'T WE JUST TALKING ABOUT THE EXAM?
FIRST PERIOD IS P.E.!
WELL, THAT WOULDN'T BE SUCH A BAD-
NO! NOT A CHANCE!

DING
DONG
TMP
TMP
TMP
TMP
YOUR TANTRUM ALMOST MADE US LATE.
YOU'RE TOO STRAIGHT-LACED, FUTARO-KUN!
YOU PLAYED HOOKY FROM THE STUDY GROUP YESTERDAY, TOO.
DON'T SLACK OFF ON ME.

PLAYED HOOKY? I HAD WORK!
AND I'M A LITTLE WORRIED ABOUT HOW EVERYTHING MOVED ALONG WITHOUT ME, TOO!
HUFF
HUFF
BARELY MADE IT...
SIGH...
NOTHING'S GOING RIGHT.
THUNK
ROAR!
MURMUR
MURMUR
MURMUR
MURMUR
?!

ICHIKA-SAN!
I SAW YOU ON THE NEWS THIS MORNING!
IS IT TRUE YOU'RE AN ACTRESS?!

I HAD NO IDEA!
WHO KNEW WE HAD SUCH A STAR IN OUR CLASS?!

WE'VE BEEN TALKING ABOUT IT ALL MORNING!
HOW FAR DID SHE GO TO GET THAT DRINK?

WAS THE MOVIE REALLY THAT BIG?
わぁあああ
WOOOOOOW!
I-I GUESS SO...

I DON'T REALLY CARE, BUT...

GOOD THING YOU AUDITIONED, HUH?
YOU'RE AN AMAZING LIAR NOW.

SHOULD I REALLY BE THIS MUCH OF A PUSH-OVER?

YOU REMEMBERED. YOU THOUGHT OF ME.

MORE THAN ANY COMPLIMENT FROM MY OTHER CLASSMATES...

EVERYONE WAS FIGHTING OVER YOU TODAY, HUH, ICHIKA?

HEY, ICHIK WE'RE GOI TO THE LIBRARY
OH, I'LL JOIN-
WHAT? I WANTED TO TALK TO YOU MORE!
CAN'T YOU STAY A LITTLE LONGER?

HAVE Y MET A CELEB TIES?
...
SORRY!
AH!
たたた TMP TMP TMP
WAIT UP, ICHIKA-CHAN!
HUH?!
WHERE'D SHE GO?

SORRY, GIRLS.

YOU'RE STILL BACK HERE?
COME ON. LET'S GO...
MIKU.

OH! SORRY.
I–
ISN'T IT KIND OF EARLY FOR IT TO GO PUBLIC?

HUH? WHAT DO YOU MEAN?
ICHIKA'S MOVIE.

DIDN'T YOU TELL ME YESTERDAY?

OH...
HE HEARD FROM MIKU...
A LOT HAS HAPPENED SINCE THEN
HE SPENDS TIME WITH EVERYONE ELSE TOO...
I GUESS THERE'S NO WAY HE'S FOCUSED ENTIRELY ON ME...

"DO AS YOU LIKE. BUT I WON'T LOSE."
"I WANT THIS LOVE TO COME TRUE EVEN IF IT MEANS DEFEATING HER."
"I DON'T WANT YOU HOLDING BACK ON ANYONE ELSE'S ACCOUNT ..."
"SO DO WHAT YOU WANT...I GUESS?"

FUTARO-KU...
FUTARO...
WHAT IS IT?
FUTARO...
I WANT TO TELL YOU SOMETHING.

ICHIKA...
...LIKES YOU.
?!

I THINK YOU'D MAKE A REALLY GREAT COUPLE.
I'LL SUPPORT YOU, OKAY?

NO, THAT...
...CAN'T BE TRUE...
IT'S TRUE.

CHAPTER 75
FIVE PAPER CRANES IN RETURN

roftbank 22:19 63%

Nakano Quintuplets (5)

Futaro-kun's birthday is in three days, right? 22:19

I was thinking about what present to get him... 22:19

But since the mock exam is coming up, wouldn't it just bother him? 22:19

Let's just forget about presents for now. 22:19

LET'S TAKE A SHORT BREAK.
AHHH, I'M SO TIRED!
WHERE'S ITSUKI-CHAN?
SHE SAID SHE HAD SOMETHING TO DO.
UESUGI-SAN, THIS QUES-TION...
!
SORRY...
I'M GONNA GO GET SOME AIR.
O-OKAY...
THUNK

DAZED
UESUGI-SAN?

WITH A LITTLE MORE TUTORING, I SHOULD BE ABLE TO BRING THEIR GRADES BACK UP TO WHERE THEY WERE.
ALTHOUGH IT ALSO DEPENDS ON HOW MUCH THEY STUDY ON THEIR OWN.
I'D LIKE TO FOCUS ON MY OWN STUDIES FOR THE MOCK EXAM, BUT I GUESS I CAN'T DO THAT...
NO, I CAN HANDLE BOTH!
I CAN SIMPLY STUDY BY MYSELF AFTER THEY LEAVE.
THEY AREN'T HOLDING ME BACK!

FUTARO?
MIKU.
TMP
TMP
TMP
...
ABOUT THE DAY AFTER TOMORROW...
ABOUT YESTER-DAY...

HUH? WHAT IS IT?
NO, YOU GO AHEAD...
I...

WHAT ARE YOU TWO TALKING ABOUT?
...
HMM?
D- DOES IT MATTER?

DO YO THINK FUTARO ALL RIGHT
HE'S FINE.
ALL WE CAN DO IS TRY TO MAKE THINGS A LITTLE EASIER FOR HIM.
SO LET'S FORGET ABOUT HIS BIRTHDAY FOR NOW. OKAY?
...OKAY.
THROB
NO REGRETS.
THIS IS HOW I CHOSE TO FIGHT.
NOW THAT I'VE TAKEN THE OTHERS OUT OF THE BATTLE, THIS IS MY CHANCE.
I'LL BE THE ONLY ONE WHO GIVES HIM A PRESENT.
I'VE GOT NO TIME TO WASTE!

AHHH, I GOT LOST ON THE WAY AND ENDED UP LATE.
!
WH-WHAT'S THAT, NINO?
HMM? THIS?

AROMA-THERAPY CANDLES THAT ARE SUPPOSED TO HELP WITH FATIGUE.
IT'S ALMOST HIS BIRTHDAY, AFTER ALL.
...OH.

WHOOPS.
THAT'S RIGHT. THIS WAS SUP-POSED TO BE A SECRET UNTIL THE DAY OF...
DIDN'T YOU READ MY MESSAGE YESTERDAY?
OH, THAT?
YEAH, I STILL WANT TO GIVE HIM MY PRESENT.
WAIT A SECOND ...
WOULDN'T THAT MEAN I'M THE ONLY ONE GIVING HIM SOME-THING?

HEH HEH!
THAT'LL MAKE IT EVEN MORE EFFECTIVE!

I FOR-GOT!
NINO'S REALLY GOING AFTER HIM!

SO?

HUH?
SO WHAT?

YOU'VE GOT ONE FOR HIM TOO, DON'T YOU?
A PRESENT.

!!
...
RUSTLE...

WE NEED TO SET SOMETHING STRAIGHT THOUGH.

ON THE LAST DAY OF THE TRIP...

I ASKED YOU TO STOP DADDY.

BUT HE SHOWED UP AT THE MEETING SPOT ANYWAY.

DO YOU HAVE ANYTHING TO SAY FOR YOURSELF?

...

OUR TASTES HAVE ALWAYS BEEN ALL OVER THE PLACE, HUH? THE FIVE OF US...

!

YES.

IT MAKES COOKING FOR EVERY-ONE A REAL PAIN IN THE BUTT.

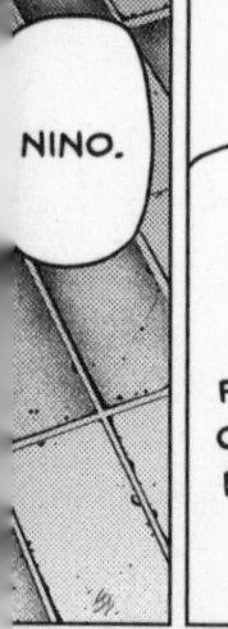

DO YOU LIKE FUTARO-KUN?
I LOVE HIM.
ME TOO.

...!
WHY DID THIS HAVE TO BE THE ONE TIME WE LIKE THE SAME THING?
I FEEL SORRY FOR YOU, NINO...

...BUT I HAVE NO INTENTION OF JUST HANDING HIM OVER.
YOU SEEM PRETTY SURE OF YOURSELF JUST BECAUSE YOU'RE OLDER.
SCENTED CANDLES AREN'T A GOOD GIFT FOR BOYS ANYWAY.
HUH?!
THAT GIFT CARD IS PRETTY CRAPPY, TOO!
WHAT'S THE PROBLEM? HE CAN USE IT TO BUY WHATEVER HE REALLY WANTS.
CRACKLE
CRACKLE
CRACKLE
CRACK
CRACK
CRACK
WHOA!!
?

WHAT ARE YOU DOING THERE, YOTSUBA?
AHAHA, YOU SURPRISED ME!
I THOUGHT UESUGI-SAN WAS BACK.
MAKING A THOUSAND PAPER CRANES!
I THOUGHT I'D MAKE THEM DURING BREAKS TO WISH FOR UESUGI-SAN TO PASS THE EXAM.
AREN'T YOU SUPPOSED TO GIVE THOSE TO SICK PEOPLE?
WELL... I HAVE HEARD THEY BRING LUCK TOO...

HE'S SEEMED PRETTY TIRED LATELY.
HE DOESN'T SAY ANYTHING, BUT STUDYING ON HIS OWN AND TEACHING US IS PRETTY HARD ON HIM.

SO I WAS HOPING I COULD AT LEAST DO SOMETHING TO HELP HIS-
OH! I DID IT!

BUT DIDN'T WE DECIDE WE WEREN'T GOING TO GIVE HIM PRESENTS?
OH.

I'M SORRY!
I DIDN'T MEAN IT LIKE THAT!
Y-YOTSUBA, THIS IS THE LIBRARY!
DON'T WORRY ABOUT IT...
I'LL NEVER ORGIVE MYSELF OR THIS!
I FEEL LIKE SUCH A CHEATER!
!
...
UH...
I BROKE OUR PROM-ISE!
I'M REALLY THE WORST!
SORRY!

LOC
A PAIR SPOR GY TICKE
I THOUGHT WE COULD TRAIN TO-GETHER...
I'VE BEEN GETTING MY PAY BY THE DAY TO BUY THEM...
SORRY FOR TRYING TO GET AN AD-VANTAGE...
YOU CAN SURE TELL WE'RE QUINTU-PLETS...

HOW ABOUT THIS?
I STILL THINK GIVING HIM THESE GIFTS BEFORE THE EXAM WILL HINDER HIS STUDIES...
SO WHY DON'T WE ALL GIVE THEM TO HIM TOGETHER, AFTER WE'RE PAST THE EXAM?
OKAY!
THAT'S THE BEST IDEA.

H-HA
ON

WHY DO YOU GET TO DECIDE THAT?
PLUS, ARE YOU EVEN OKAY WITH THAT YOURSELF?
...NONE OF YOU UNDER-STAND FU-TARO-KUN.

HOW ABOUT THIS?!

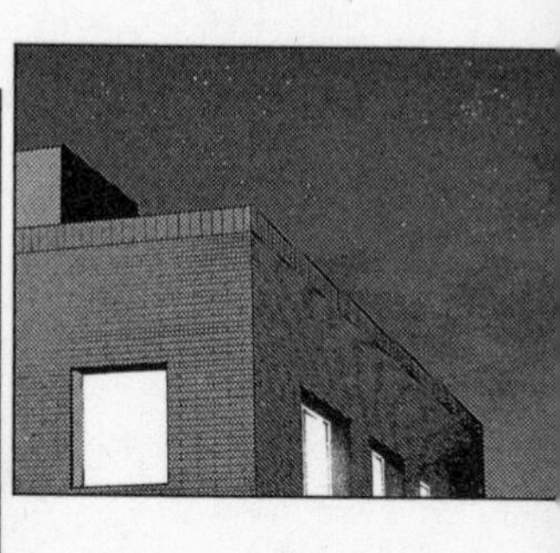

NOD
NOD

SO YO HAVEN GONE HOME YET?
I CAN'T BELIEVE YOU'RE STUDYING THIS LATE.
CLINK

SINCE YOU INSIST ON PUSHING YOURSELF SO HARD...
I BROUGHT YOU REFRESH-MENTS.
ITSUKI...

WHAT ARE YO TALKIN ABOUT
I'M NOT PUSHING MYSELF.
GLUG
GLUG
WHO DO YOU THINK I AM?

THE OTHER DAY, I WENT TO A CRAM SCHOOL INSTRUC-TOR NAMED SHIMODA-SAN.

!

I AM NOT CERTAIN YOU COULD CALL IT A PART-TIME JOB, BUT...
I PLAN TO FURTHER INCREASE MY ACADEMIC SKILLS WHILE ASSISTING SHIMODA-SAN.

SO I'M NOT GOOD ENOUGH?

DON'T POUT.
HAT'S NOT VHAT SAID.

FOR THE SAKE OF MY DREAMS BEYOND THE MOCK EXAM... BEYOND GRADUATION...
I WANT TO SEE AN EDUCATOR IN ACTION.

...
I REALLY AN'T PREDICT WHAT OU GIRLS RE GONNA O NEXT...

SINCE THE NEW TERM STARTED...
YOTSUBA...
NINO...
ICHIKA...
...
AND EVEN MIKU...
HMM?
HAS OMETHING HING APENED ITH-

!
I'LL TELL YOU... ONE DAY...

BZZZZ
BZZZT
BZZZT

NN...
WHEN DID I FALL...
FWIP...
OH.
From Raiha
When are you gonna be home, big brother? We're waiting to start your birthday party!
RIGHT. THAT WAS TODAY.
GUESS I'LL HEAD HOME.
!

FIVE... PAPER CRANES?
?

WHAT THE?
WHAT KIND OF PAPER IS THIS...?
!
RUSTLE
RUSTLE
Nino
Yotsuba
Itsuki
Ichika
Miku

I GUESS I'M NOT ALONE...
THEY'RE WORKING HARD TOO.
I CAN'T LET THEM SHOW ME UP.

CHAPTER 76
THE MEN'S BATTLE

YOU'VE GOTTA HURRY OR YOU'RE GONNA BE LATE FOR SCHOOL, BIG BROTHER!
JUST FIVE MORE MIN-UTES...
JUST LET ME REVIEW FOR FIVE MORE MINUTES...
JEEZ! PULL IT TOGETHER! DON'T YOU HAVE A MAJOR TEST TODAY?!

HERE! EAT THI BREAD
IS THIS MY LIMIT?
WHAP
WHAP
I'M OFF!
YOU CAN DO IT!
GIVE 'EM HELL, SON!
OH?
RAIHA...

WHERE'D MY MILK GO?
HUH?
DID BIG BROTHER TAKE THAT ONE?
SLUUURP
licious Milk
GOOD MORNING.

FLOP...
IT'S FINALLY THE DAY OF THE EXAM.
LET'S ALL DO OUR BEST!
WOW, THOSE BAGS UNDER YOUR EYES ARE RIDIC-ULOUS.
YOU'RE ONE TO TALK.
SO? THINK YOU CAN GET INTO THE TOP TEN?

OF COURSE...
HA HA HA HA!
UESUGI-KUN!
FIRST OFF, ALLOW ME TO PRAISE YOU FOR COMING HERE INSTEAD OF RUNNING AWAY!
HIM AGAIN...
BUT I'M SURE YOU WILL RUE THIS DAY!
YOU WILL RUE THAT YOU DID NOT RUN WHEN YOU HAD THE CHANCE!

IT'S TOO EARLY FOR THIS...
UESUGI-SAN WON'T LOSE!

I'M NOT TALKING TO YOU!

...
HAS HE ALWAYS BEEN LIKE THIS?
UESUGI-KUN.
THIS IS OUR FINAL SHOWDOWN...

WE SHALL SETTLE THINGS ONCE AND FOR ALL, MAN-TO-MAN...
WISH

HURRY UP, GIRLS.
THERE'S STILL TIME BEFORE IT STARTS.
WE MUST STRUGGLE UNTIL THE VERY END.

OKAY!
...

SORRY. IT'S NOT MAN-TO-MAN.

THERE ARE SIX OF US HERE.
HEH HEH HEH...

TIC!
PLEASE EMPTY YOUR DESKS AN TAKE YOU SEATS.
KEEP YOUR PAPERS FACE DOWN UNTIL I GIVE YOU THE SIGNAL.
TIC
WE WILL NOW BEGIN THE NATIONAL MOCK EXAM.
...
OH NO...
NO, I CAN STILL DO THIS!
I WILL DO IT!

DING
DONG
PHEW, THAT'S ONE SUBJECT DOWN!
LAN-GUAGE ARTS IS TOUGH!

AREN'T YOU A LIT-TLE PALE, FUTARO-KUN?
D-DON'T WORRY ABOUT IT.
HOW'D YOU DO, TAKEDA?

I'M SURE IT WAS NO PROBLEM FOR THIS GUY.
YEAH, I'LL BET YOU GOT A PER-FECT 200, RIGHT?
HAHA! I DON'T KNOW.

CHINESE LIT DID GIVE ME A LITTLE TROU-BLE. I MAY HAVE MISSED AT LEAST ONE QUESTION.
UDE... EVEN ISSING NLY ONE PLENTY NCREDI-BLE...

I GUESS THAT MEANS TAKEDA'LL BE NUMBER ONE IN THE SCHOOL AGAIN, HUH?
SO YOU WERE SIMPLY A BIG FISH IN A SMALL POND?

HMM?
YOU SAY SOME-THING?
VZZZT
ブルルル
You have a new message.
From: Father
Yusuke,
Come to the chairman's office immediately.
GALASSIA
Chairman

YUSUKE...
I JUST TOOK A LOOK AT YOUR ANSWERS FOR THE PREVIOUS SUBJECT.
YOU MOVE FAST.
AND HERE ARE THE AN-SWERS FOR THE EXAM I ARRANGED TO GET.
!

THREE ANSWERS INCORRECT.
190 POINTS.

WHAT? BUT!
DO YOU REALLY BELIEVE YOU CAN MEET DOCTOR NAKANO'S EXPECTATIONS WITH A SCORE LIKE THIS?

SINCE YOU WERE SMALL, YOU'VE BEEN SAYING YOU WANTED TO BECOME A DOCTOR LIKE YOUR MOTHER.
THE RESULTS OF THIS EXAM COULD EARN YOU A LOT OF CREDIT WITH DOCTOR NAKANO.
YOU MUST GET RESULTS HERE.

FATHER... I...
YUSUKE.
FWIP
!

DON'T WORRY YOUR POOR FATHER.

PHEW!
IT'S FINALLY LUNCH-TIME!
ONLY TWO SUBJECTS LEFT! HANG IN THERE, EVERYBODY!
TIME TO EAT AFTER ALL THAT TEST-TAKING, YES!
FUTARO'S HEAD WAS DROOP-ING... I HOPE HE'S OKAY...
ALL WE CAN DO NOW IS TRUST HIM.
OR ELSE...
...WE CAN'T GIVE HIM THE PRES-ENTS WE READIED.
HUH?
WHERE IS UESUGI-SAN ANYWAY?
OH... UH...
HE WENT TO THE BATH-ROOM AND HASN'T COME BACK.
GURGLE URGLE URGLE
WHY DID IT HAVE TO BE TODAY?
TALK ABOUT BAD LUCK...
SHHHH
CHACK

HEY THERE.
YOU WERE CERTAINLY IN THERE FOR A WHILE.
YOU KNOW, I KIND OF THOUGHT YOU WERE OUT HERE.

WHY NOT SPEND YOUR TIME REVIEWING INSTEAD OF WASTING IT HERE?
REVIEW? HEH HEH...
OT NEC-ESSARY.

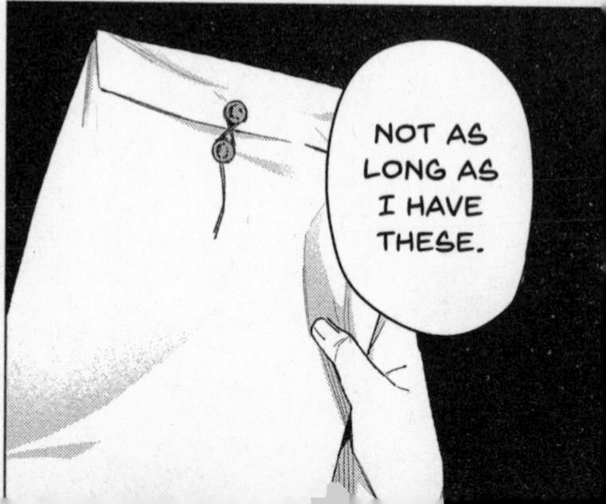
NOT AS LONG AS I HAVE THESE.

?

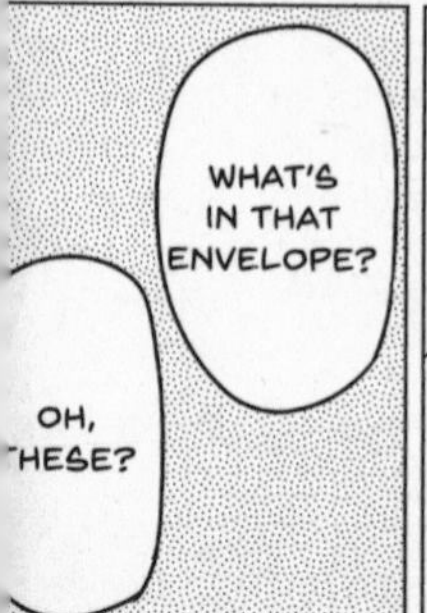
WHAT'S IN THAT ENVELOPE?
OH, HESE?

THESE ARE THE ANSWERS FOR THE MOCK EXAM.
EVERY LAST ONE OF THEM IS CONTAINED WITHIN.
?!

HOW DID YOU GET THOSE?
I MEAN, YOU HAV THOSE, THEN–
EXACT-LY.

MY VIC-TORY IS ASSURED.
NO MATTER HOW EX-CELLENT YOUR SCORE.

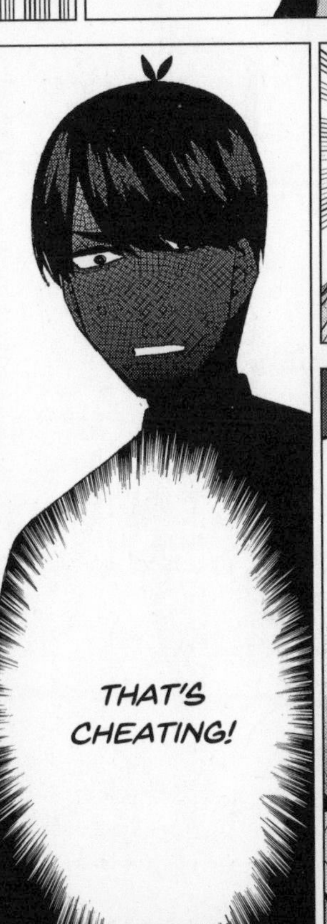
THAT'S CHEATING!

IF THAT'S TRUE, HE'S MORE OR LESS GUARANTEED A PERFECT SCORE.
THEN I'LL HAVE TO GET EVERY QUESTION RIGHT TOO...
CAN I DO THAT?!

SHRRRP

SHRP
SHRP
SHRP
SHRP

WHUMP
RELAX. I DIDN'T OPEN THAT ENVE-LOPE DURING THE MORNING SECTIONS EITHER.
YOU–
UESUGI-KUN, I...
Please
Only flush toilet paper.
ZSHHH

...WANT TO BE AN ASTRO-NAUT.
HMM?
WHAT?
COULD YOU EXPLAIN THAT FROM THE BEGINNING, PLEASE?
I'VE ALWAYS LONGED TO BE THERE, WHERE THERE IS NO GROUND, NO SKY, NOT EVEN ANY AIR.
THERE'S NOTHING...AND THEREFORE EVERYTHING!
OKAY. SCRATCH THE EXPLANA-TION.

IT'S THE ONE PATH OUT OF TH RESTRAINE LIFE I WA BORN INT
I KNOW THAT IT IS A HARD PATH.

ONLY A SELECT HANDFUL OF PEOPLE EVER MAKE IT TO SPACE.
EVERY-ONE ON EARTH IS MY RIVAL.

THAT IS WHY I CANNOT LOSE HERE...
...IN THIS TINY SCHOOL... IN THIS TINY COUNTRY.

THIS IS MY DREAM.

I SHALL DEFEAT YOU WITH MY OWN POWER!
A RESULT ACHIEVED THROUGH UNDER-HANDED METHODS HAS NO MEANING!
URGLE-
URGLE-
URGLE-
URGLE
UGH!!
HUNK
ACK
...
HEH!
TAKEDA.

I'LL ACCEPT THAT CHAL- LENGE.
HAHAHA! WHAT ARE YOU SAYING?
OF COURSE YOU WILL! WE ARE ETERNAL RIVALS!

SIR.
WE JUST RECEIVED THE RESULTS OF LAST MONTH'S MOCK EXAM.

EXCELLENT WORK.

TUMP

THE GIRLS, THOUGH THERE IS SOME INDIVIDUAL VARIANCE, HAVE GREATLY IMPROVED UPON THEIR SCORES FROM LAST YEAR.

k Exa

Na

Name	National Rank
Ichika Nakano	146,079/25

Subject Score	Possible
English	70/200

I BELIEVE WE CAN CONSIDER THE PRIVATE TUTOR PLAN A GREAT SUCCESS.
ALTHOUGH, NATURALLY, THE GIRLS' OWN EFFORTS WERE VITAL AS WELL.

TAKEDA-SAMA SUCCESSFULLY ACHIEVED THE NATIONAL RANK OF 8TH.

National Mock Exam

Name	National Ran
Yusuke Takeda	8/250,762

Subject Score	Possibl
English	189/2(
Math	192/2(

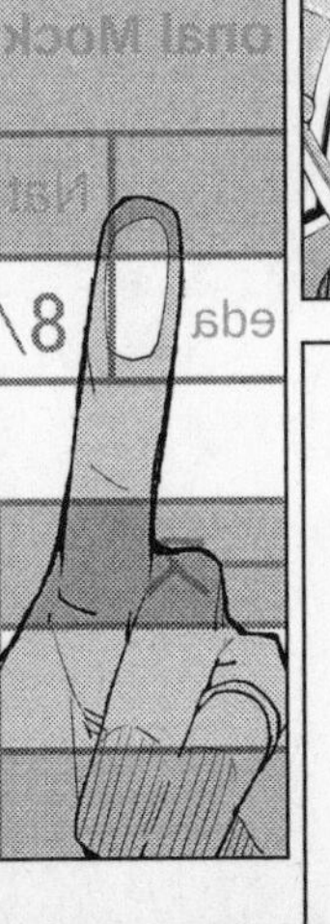

#3.
IT IS BAD NEW AS FAR AS YOU ARE CONCERNED, SIR...
...BUT THINGS PLAYED OUT EXACTLY AS HE PROCLAIMED.
IT'S AN ODD-LOOKING ANSWER SHEET, ISN'T IT?
HIS SCORE FOR THE FIRST FOUR SUBJECTS IS PERFECT. NOT A SINGLE WRONG ANSWER.
BUT FOR THE LAST SUBJECT, HE TURNED IN HIS ANSWER SHEET WITH THE LAST FEW QUESTIONS LEFT BLANK.
ACCORDING TO THE REPORTS, HE COLLAPSED INTO A DEEP SLEEP OUT OF THE BLUE.
HE MAY HAVE STRAINED HIMSELF TOO MUCH IN HIS STUDIES.

BUT...
...IF HE HAD BEEN ABLE TO ANSWER THOSE LAST FEW QUESTIONS...
"FIRST PLACE ON THE NATIONAL MOCK EXAM!"

WHO CAN SAY FOR CERTAIN?
THERE'S NO POINT IN THINKING ABOUT THAT NOW.

FUTARO UESUGI... HE GETS IN MY WAY AT EVERY TURN.
EVERY TIME HE BECOMES INVOLVED, MY PLANS GO AWRY.
HONESTLY... WHAT A PAIN.
BUT HIS COMMIT-MENT...

...IS
ADMIRA-
BLE.

CHAPTER 77
THE WOMEN'S BATTLE
ADMIRA-BLE.
I DON'T KNOW WHAT ELSE TO CALL IT.

I APPROACHED THE MOCK EXAM WITH THE INTENTION OF DEFEATING YOU EVEN IF YOU PLACED IN THE TOP TEN.
ギコ
SKREEK
ギコ
SKREEK
#8 IS A RANK I NORMALLY NEVER WOULD HAVE EVEN HOPED FOR.

SKREEK
ギコ
ギコ
SKREEK
I CAN'T BELIEVE YOU SURPASSED EVEN THAT.

CONGRATU-LATIONS ON REACHING #3.
ギコ
SKREEK
SKREEK
ギコ
IT IS ALMOST TIME FOR THE FIELD TRIP, SO–
WAIT A SECOND.

TELL ME WHY I'M SWING-ING WITH YOU ON THIS PLAYGROUND IN THE MIDDLE OF THE DAY.
YAY!
YAY!
HAHA! YESTERDAY'S ENEMY IS TODAY'S FRIEND.
THIS MAY BE WHAT YOUTH IS ALL ABOUT.
I'M LEAVING.
THWUMP
OH, NOT BAD.
THUMP
CLANK
CLANK
NOT GOOD ENOUGH YET, EH?
WELL, DON'T RUSH THINGS.
HAVE YOU FORGOT-TEN?
WE WERE ASKED HERE.
SEE?
HE HAS ARRIVED.
SKREEK

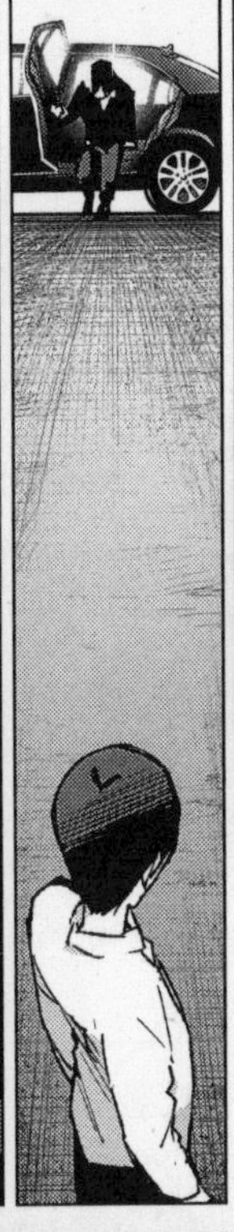

I APOLO-GIZE FOR THE WAIT.

FIRST, TAKEDA-K CONGRAT LATIONS COMING 8TH NATIC WIDE.
I AM SURE YOUR FATHER IS QUITE PROUD OF HAVING A SON LIKE YOU.

I HEAR YOU ARE AIMING TO BECOME A DOCTOR.

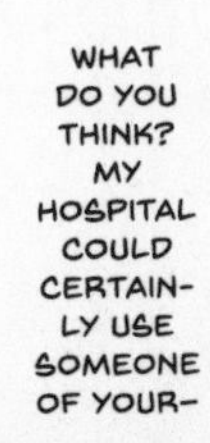
WHAT DO YOU THINK? MY HOSPITAL COULD CERTAIN-LY USE SOMEONE OF YOUR-

I'M TERRIBLY SORRY.
I AM HONORED YOU WOULD EVEN CONSIDER ME...
...BUT I WISH TO THINK ON MY FUTURE COURSE OF ACTION A LITTLE LONGER.
I SEE. THEN I WILL HOPE YOU EVENTUALLY DECIDE IN MY FAVOR.
UESUGI-KUN.
ES?

I WISH TO HIRE YOU TO ONCE AGAIN TUTOR MY DAUGHTERS.

THE PAY IS FIVE TIMES THE MARKET RATE.
IT'S A VERY HOMEY, FUN WORKPLACE.
YES, I KNOW THE PLACE VERY WELL.

HUH?!

TO BE PERFECT FRANK, DON'T LI THE IDEA REHIRIN YOU.

THIS JOB IS TOO MUCH EVEN FOR MOST PROS.

BUT...

I HEAR YOU'RE THE ONLY ONE WHO CAN DO IT.
WANT THE JOB?
!

OF COURS
I WAS PLANNING TO DO IT ANYWAY!
IF I'LL GET PAID FOR MY WORK, ALL THE BETTER!

EXCELLENT. THEN AS WE INITIALLY DISCUSSED, THE JOB WILL LAST ALL THE WAY THROUGH-
OH.
ACTUALLY, I'D LIKE TO TELL YOU SOMETHING RELATED TO THAT.

IF WE'RE TALKING ONLY ABOUT THEIR ABILITY TO GRADUATE, I THINK YOUR DAUGHTERS ARE ALREADY AT THE NECESSARY LEVEL.

I THOUGHT THAT WAS ALL THEY NEEDED.
BUT AFTER LISTENING TO ITSUKI...
...AND THIS GUY, TAKEDA, I CHANGED MY MIND.

IT'S NOT A TRUE GRADUATION UNLESS THEY DISCOVER THEIR NEXT PATH IN LIFE.
I WANT TO HELP THEM FIND THEIR DREAMS.

UESUGI-KUN...
...

YOU'VE CHANGED QUITE A BIT.
IT'S HARD TO IMAGINE YOU'RE THE SAME PERSON WHO WAS BEGRUDGINGLY PERFORMING THIS JOB AT THE BEGINNING.
-YOU KNEW
UT THAT?

WHATEVER APPROACH YOU EMPLOY IS YOUR OWN CHOICE. I DON'T EVEN THINK YOU ARE WRONG.
RMB
RMB
RMB

UT I WANT
OU TO KEEP
NE THING IN
MIND...
RMB
RMB

...YOU ARE THEIR TUTOR AND NOTHING MORE. I TRUST YOU WILL BEHAVE CHIVALROUSLY TOWARD MY DAUGHTERS.
O-OF COURSE! I'VE DRAWN A LINE IN THE SAND!
I HAVE... REALLY!
HAHA. HAHAHA...
VROOM
I GUESS HE...
...DOES ACTUALLY WORRY ABOUT THEM...
VWOOM
HUH?!

U-UESUGI-KUN...
WAS THAT OUR FATHER'S CAR YOU STEPPED OUT OF?

WH-WHAT WERE...
UHHH... WELL...

I'M RETURNING TO MY POST AS YOUR TUTOR.
!
BEAM

THEN HE FINALLY AC-KNOWL-EDGED YOUR HARD WORK!
CON-GRATU...
HUH?!

WHY ARE YOU AVOIDING ME?
BECAUSE OF YOUR FATHER'S STERN TALKING-TO...
'T EVEN WITHOUT IT, I NEED TO ETHINK THE DIS-ANCE I MAINTAIN ETWEEN MYSELF ID THE GIRLS SO) ONE GETS ANY FUNNY IDEAS.

ALTHOUGH...I THINK WOR-RYING ABOUT THIS SISTER IN PARTICULAR IS PROBABLY A WASTE OF TIME.
VERY SUSPI-CIOUS...

CHACK

OH! WELCOME, UESUGI-SAN!
YOU FINALLY SHOWED UP!
YOU'RE LATE. WHAT WERE YOU DOING?

WAIT! WHOA!
WHAT'S ALL THIS?!
AHAHA!
SINCE THINGS FINALLY SET-TLED DOWN A BIT, WE WERE DOING SOME CLEANING.

WEREN'T GOING REVIEW EXAM?
HEY! DID YOU USE THE ARO-MATHERAPY STUFF?
HUH?
YOU KNOW, THE ONES I GAVE YOU.
YOUR BIRTHDAY PRESENT.

OH, AROMA-THERAPY, RIGHT? YEAH, ISN'T IT GREAT.
YES, YES. AROMATHER-APY.
IT'S NOT FOR EVERYONE, BUT I THINK AROMATHERAPY IS DELICIOUS.
YOU'VE GOT NO IDEA WHAT THAT IS, DO YOU?
YEESH! I'LL TELL YOU HOW, SO JUST USE THEM.
TARO-KUN, ABOUT MY RESENT...
OH YEAH... YOURS WAS KIND OF DIF-FERENT, HUH?
I'M SUPPOSED TO GO SHOPPING WITH THAT?
YEP!
THAT'LL BE A HUGE HELP!
THANKS, ICHIKA!
I WISH I'D THOUGHT OF THAT...
HOW DID YOU LIKE MY GIFT?
I'LL BET IF YOU BOUGHT SOMETHING FOR RAIHA-CHAN WITH IT, SHE'D LOVE IT.
AWE-SOME!
HEH HEH HEH...
OH YEAH, I'M IM-PRESSED YOU MADE SO-
...

OH...
IT DOESN'T LOOK LIKE WE'LL GET ANY WORK DONE TODAY...
SO I THINK I'LL GO HOME.

WHAT? ALREADY?
WHY DON'T YOU AT LEAST TAKE A BREAK BEFORE YOU LEAVE?

SIGH...

CREEEAAAK...
I SMELL SOMEONE KEEPING SECRETS.

I FELT IT IN MY BONES!
ARE YOU HIDING SOMETHING FROM ME?

DID FATHER TELL YOU SOMETHING A-
O-OF COURSE NOT!

GRRR...

THEN LET'S TRY THIS!
IF YOU TELL ME WHAT YOU ARE HIDING, I WILL TELL YOU ONE THING I AM HIDING AS WELL.
?
SOMETHING YOU'RE HIDING?
I'M NOT REALLY INTERESTED...
WHA?!
AW, COME ON! WHY NOT?!
I CAN'T KEEP IT IN ANY LONGER.
BUT THIS IS THE ONLY WAY I CAN FORCE MYSELF TO SAY IT...
OKAY, MAYBE THIS IS A GOOD OPPORTUNITY.
THEN I'LL TELL YOU. DON'T GET CREEPED OUT.
OF OURSE!

I'M SUD-DENLY REALLY POPULAR WITH GIRLS...
WHOA...

OH, I'M JUST GETTING STARTED. THE GIRLS THAT CAN' RESIST ME ARE NONE OTHER THA NINO AND ICHIKA.

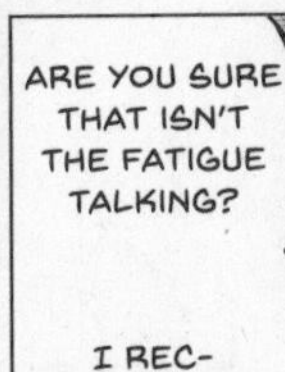
ARE YOU SURE THAT ISN'T THE FATIGUE TALKING?

I REC-OMMEND PLENTY OF REST.

WAIT, NINO AND ICHIKA?

NOT MIKU?
!

NO, NOT HER.

MIKU AND YOTSUBA SAID THEY'D SUPPORT US.
WHAT DO THEY WANT ME TO DO...?

MIKU AND YOTSUBA ARE...
...SUP-PORTING YOU...
HEY.

I TOLD YOU A PRETTY EMBARRASSING ONE.
YOU'D BETTER TELL ME AN EQUALLY EMBARRASSING ONE FAST.
A-ALL RIGHT!
A-
ACTUALLY...

...I HAVE ANOTHER FACE.

!
ONE I CANNOT REVEAL TO ANYONE...
ONE I'VE KEPT SECRET FOR AGES...
YOU CAN'T MEAN...
I AM-
I'LL GO FIND ITSUKI!
HUH?! OH, YOU WERE JUST TALKING TO UESUGI-SAN.
ICHIKA'S TRYING TO FIGURE OUT WHOSE BOX THAT IS IN THE CLOSET...
ERE YOU IN THE IDDLE OF SOME-THING?

SHE WAS JUST ABOUT TO TELL AN EMBARRASSING SECRET.
WOW!
I-I'M SORRY! I WILL TELL YOU SOME OTHER TIME!
H-HEY! NO FAIR! I TOLD YOU MINE!
TMP
TMP
TMP
OH... I GUESS I MESSED THINGS UP, HUH?
WELL, I'VE GOT A PRETTY GOOD IDEA WHAT SHE WAS GONNA SAY.
YOTSUBA...
HAVE YOU HEARD OF THE FAMOUS REVIEWER M-A-Y?

HEY, MIKU!
WELCOME BACK FROM WORK!
NICE TIMING, YOTSUBA.
YOU'RE WORKING HARD EVERY DAY LATELY!
HEY, DID YOU KNOW THIS? ITSUKI'S ACTUALLY-
TRY THIS BREAD...
...I BAKED.

DO YOU RECOGNIZE THIS BOX, ITSUKI-CHAN?
I-IT'S MINE.
I PUT SOME CLOTHES I DIDN'T THINK I WOULD WEAR AGAIN INSIDE.
IF YOU DON'T NEED THEM, LET'S OSS 'EM OUT.
..ALTHOUGH I GUESS 'VE GOT NO ROOM TO TALK.
FWIP
ス
!

ITSUKI-CHAN, YOU DROPPED SOME-

I CAN'T LET THEM BEAT ME.

IT'S ALMOST TIME FOR THE BIGGEST EVENT IN HIGH SCHOOL...
...THE FIELD TRIP.
THIS IS MY BIGGEST CHANCE TO GET FU-KUN'S ATTENTION.

THE FIELD TRIP... WE'RE GOING THERE AGAIN?

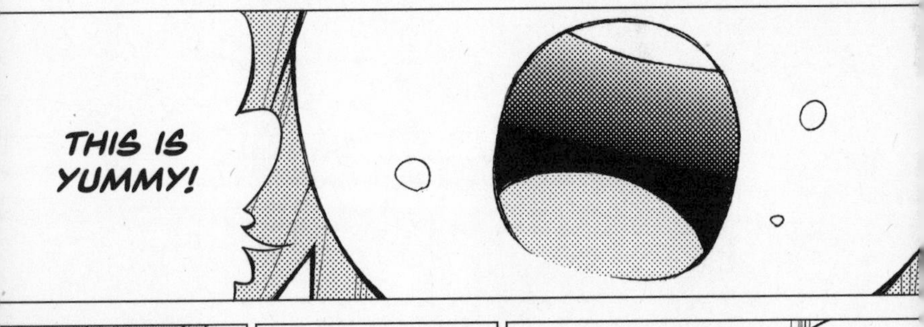
THIS IS YUMMY!

DID YOU REALLY MAKE THIS, MIKU?!
IT'S REALLY DELICIOUS!
I'VE BEEN TRAINING.
IF ONLY YOU GOT HERE A FEW MINUTES SOONER!
UESUGI-SAN WAS JUST HERE!
I'LL WAIT JUST A LITTLE BIT LONGER...

I WANT FUTARO TO TRY IT IN THE PERFECT SETTING.
BY THE WAY, WHAT DO YOU MEAN BY "PERFECT"?
YOU KNOW, THAT PLACE IN KYOTO WHERE-

THIS IS...
...IN
YOTO...

OH, I GET IT.
I JUST CAN'T... TELL HIM...
WHAT HAPPENED IN KYOTO...
AND... HOW CAN I EVER EXPLAIN THIS?

Field Trips
in Kyoto
THE FIELD TRIP.
OUR DESTINATION, KYOTO.

THIS IS WHERE I'LL SETTLE THINGS.

CONTINUED IN VOLUME 10!

THE QUINTUPLETS CANNOT SHARE THEIR HEIGHT EVENLY

THE QUINTUPLETS CANNOT SHARE A BATHROOM EVENLY

Staff Ueno Hino Cho Erimura Naito

Something's Wrong With Us

NATSUMI ANDO

The dark, psychological, sexy shojo series readers have been waiting for!

A spine-chilling and steamy romance between a Japanese sweets maker and the man who framed her mother for murder!

Following in her mother's footsteps, Nao became a traditional Japanese sweets maker, and with unparalleled artistry and a bright attitude, she gets an offer to work at a world-class confectionary company. But when she meets the young, handsome owner, she recognizes his cold stare...

PERFECT WORLD

Rie Aruga

An office party reunites Tsugumi with her high school crush Itsuki. He's realized his dream of becoming an architect, but along the way, he experienced a spinal injury that put him in a wheelchair. Now Tsugumi's rekindled feelings will butt up against prejudices she never considered — and Itsuki will have to decide if he's ready to let someone into his heart...

"Depicts with great delicacy and courage the difficulties some with disabilities experience getting involved in romantic relationships... Rie Aruga refuses to romanticize, pushing her heroine to face the reality of disability. She invites her readers to the same tasks of empathy, knowledge and recognition."
—Slate.fr

"An important entry [in manga romance]... The emotional core of both plot and characters indicates thoughtfulness... [Aruga's] research is readily apparent in the text and artwork, making this feel like a real story."
—Anime News Network

A Kodansha Comics Trade Paperback Original

Published in the United States by Kodansha Comics, an imprint of Kodansha USA Publishing, LLC, New York.

Publication rights for this English edition arranged through Kodansha Ltd., Tokyo.

First published in Japan in 2019 by Kodansha Ltd., Tokyo as *Gotoubun no hanayome*, volume 9.

ISBN 978-1-63236-920-8

Cover Design: Saya Takagi (RedRooster)

Printed in the United States of America.

www.kodanshacomics.com

9 8 7 6 5 4 3 2 1
Translation: Steven LeCroy
Lettering: Jan Lan Ivan Concepcion
Additional Layout: Belynda Ungurath
Editorial Assistance: YKS Services LLC/SKY Japan, INC.
Kodansha Comics edition cover design by Phil Balsman

Publisher: Kiichiro Sugawara
Vice president of marketing & publicity: Naho Yamada

Director of publishing services: Ben Applegate
Associate director of operations: Stephen Pakula
Publishing services managing editor: Noelle Webster
Assistant production manager: Emi Lotto, Angela Zurlo